THE
STUDY
SECRET

Inspiration for *The Study Secret*

A few years ago, I was so astonished to learn that a recent research study funded by the Bill and Melinda Gates Foundation had found that only 54% of all students who enter a college or university in the United States actually graduate with a degree within six years. And when that statistic is broken down further into sub-populations, the numbers are even more dismal. For example, 42% of Hispanic students and only 37% of African American students graduate with a degree within that same time period (*The American Dream Report 2.0, 2013*).

Another important study conducted by Public Agenda called "With Their Whole Lives Ahead of Them—Myths and Realities About Why So Many Students Fail to Finish College" took on the question of *why* so many students drop out before completing their degree. It identified the main reason as the conflict students experience between school, work and family commitments. Interestingly, of those students who dropped out 23% reported spending too much time socializing and not enough time studying (Johnson and Rochkind, 2009).

As an educator, my heart was touched because I genuinely had no idea that the college graduation rates were that low and why so many students drop out. I asked myself what I could do to help as many students as possible make that degree a reality, so I wrote *The Study Secret* with that goal in mind.

*This book is dedicated to my parents, family, friends,
teachers, mentors, colleagues, and students
who all taught me more than they will ever know.*

CONTENTS

INTRODUCTION

Years ago I stepped onto a college campus for the first time with a fairly common outlook on the years ahead of me. You see, school had always come easy to me. I'd mostly skated by in high school, and I entered my university believing the same would be true there. I would go to classes, make good grades without even trying, work a part-time job and still have plenty of time leftover for socializing and partying.

I was an idiot.

If you're reading this book now, you've probably already come to realize what I did all those years ago. You've gone to the parties, made friends with your dorm mates, run across campus after waking up late for your morning class, and groaned in defeat when your first (or second) round of tests and project grades were posted.

You've had to admit to yourself that this whole college thing isn't as easy as you thought.

Or maybe you never thought it would be easy. Maybe it's been a major battle just to get to college, and now that you are here, it's a totally new experience. But you're here now, in college, because you've worked hard to be here. Because you wanted it (or at least, thought you did). And maybe you're struggling to keep your head above water, panicking at the realization that college is turning out to be even harder than you expected.

Breathe.

You are not alone. Everything about this new stage of your

life is exciting and challenging, scary and overwhelming, all at the same time. Whether you know it, every other student lined up in those dorms or sitting in those classrooms beside you is struggling in some way themselves. It's hard to balance school life, work life, family life, and still have a decent social life with friends.

It's kind of a universal experience.

Of course, knowing you're not alone doesn't exactly make it any easier to swallow the fact that you're basically drowning in the pre-reqs, the ones you have to finish before moving onto coursework you're actually interested in (because let's be honest, no one really wants to be in Calc 101.) The knowledge that everyone's struggling doesn't make you feel better about your parents hounding you to be deserving of the education they're paying for, or giving you a hard time about going to a party instead of staying home to study.

It doesn't change the fact that none of this has been what you thought it would be.

But I'm here to tell you—it can be.

And if you are about to start college, then consider yourself lucky to receive this hack to college life—great grades, the cool social life, and a balanced living—before experiencing the big struggle that keeps about half of all students from graduating with a degree!

The Study Secret can revolutionize the way you study, allowing you to digest more information in less time and cutting hours off your old, conventional study habits so that you have time to dedicate elsewhere. That means more time to socialize, party with your friends, do extra-curricular activities, work that job, and focus on just about anything else that matters to you, while still getting better grades than you are now.

I'm excited to tell you that the quality of your college experience *can* get better. You *can* have less stress and a more productive, balanced college life. You can have it all . . . if you have a system.

The Study Secret gives you a practical system that anyone can follow. It's composed of eight power habits working together to make any college student more successful, no matter what your past experience has been.

This system is how I made it through. How I ultimately graduated with straight A's and Magna Cum Laude honors, all while working 30 hours a week and enjoying a wonderful social life, too. I made it past the initial struggle by practicing some essential power habits I'm going to share with you here in this book—power habits that will allow you to experience success in all your classes *and* have time for a great social life and any other activities important to you.

So I know what you're thinking. "Power habits" sounds like some term you might hear on a late-night infomercial and then later make fun of with your friends. While any one of these habits will help you individually, their true power is best harnessed when you practice them all together. It's when you get to fully experience their synergistic effect that takes you to the top of your game!

Synergy is the interaction of elements that when combined produce a total effect that is greater than the sum of the individual elements, contributions, etc. (Dictionary.com)

But I'm telling you, these are the habits you absolutely need — the habits that will not only help you to start pulling grades you can be proud of, but that will also free up more time for you to actually enjoy that social life, the one you didn't exactly tell your parents you mostly came to college for.

It's okay . . . I was there once myself. I get it.

Here's something you should know about me, though: I now see myself as a lifelong learner who pursues and enjoys learning and experiencing new things all the time, and I truly believe you can be, too. That everyone can be, and should be. Once I figured out how to stay ahead in my classes, I found I actually really loved being there. So much so that I went on to pursue my master's degree and to spend several years teaching: a career that allowed me to work with a lot of students.

A lot of students like you.

Smart, capable students, who wanted to do well, but didn't always know how to unlock all of that hidden potential.

Let me tell you, it's there inside you. And you are absolutely capable of succeeding in college, even beyond what you thought was possible. You are capable of making your parents proud and earning the degree that will set you up for a career you've been dreaming of. You just have to believe in yourself and be willing to change some habits first.

These eight power habits are a collection of best practices that essentially guarantee your academic success. In fact, most successful college students are already using some of them. But my bet is, if you're struggling with the whole "school-family-friends-work" life balance and getting a study system down that really works for you (and cramming doesn't count), you just haven't figured out how to use the eight power habits all together for some serious synergy that truly allows you to have it all.

Ready to hear me out now?

Here's a brief preview of what these power habits are. They may look simple, but I want you to read this list with an open mind and allow me to shed some light on each one before you shrug it off or assume you know what it's all about. I promise you will be surprised!

1. Create A Success Plan
2. Make Attendance Mandatory
3. Connect With Your Professors
4. Smart Scheduling
5. Power Reading
6. Hack Your Notes
7. The BrainChat Study Method
8. Seek A Balanced Life

By the way, I can almost guarantee you haven't yet embraced

that seventh one — the BrainChat Study Method — which will be the key to piecing it all together!

The decision to seek education beyond high school is no doubt one of the best choices you can make for yourself, whether you are attending a vocational college, local community college, four-year university, online institution, or post-graduate program. And regardless of why you're in school (whether it was something you truly wanted, or something your parents kind of pushed on you), the months and years ahead hold so much potential for the rest of your life.

And here is the big *why* to that last statement: College catches you during the most formative years of young adulthood and prepares and processes you in a way that makes you a better, more useful person no matter what you choose to study or in whichever field you choose to work.

Still, school is a huge personal commitment and a significant investment of your time and money, even if it's someone else's money currently funding your tuition. Unfortunately, too many students undertake their higher education without a thoroughly conceived success plan in place. As a result, many fail or drop out before they ever have a chance to succeed.

Plenty of students give up when it turns out college is harder than they thought it would be, because honestly it's not the college part by itself; it's the college part plus everything else they have going on in their lives.

But I don't want that to be you.

I believe that the BrainChat Study Method and the power habits that go with it are the very best method of studying for success. In fact, this whole system is one of the most effective ways to process, learn and retain the vast amounts of information your professors are already throwing at you. (And I'm not just talking about quick memorization for a test). Why? Because it matches the way your brain likes to learn.

As you begin to incorporate all the power habits I'm going to break down for you in the pages to come, you will find that this whole system can shave hours off the traditional ways students study. Ultimately, that means more time for you to go on those dates, to eat out with your friends, to hit up that party, or perhaps to get a job that will help pay for everything you want to do.

Yes, you can have the college experience you've always dreamed of and pull off the grades that will pave the way for a brighter future.

But it all starts with a plan . . .

1. CREATE YOUR SUCCESS PLAN

What if I asked you to tell me why you're in college? To really think about it, and to explain what your ultimate goals for being here are. How would you respond?

Some of you would tell me about your childhood dreams of becoming a teacher, or doctor, or other professional, and you would explain that you are here now because earning that degree is necessary to become what you've always wanted to be when you grew up.

Others would admit they don't really know what they want to be when they grow up (and that's perfectly okay, too—not many people do in their late teens and early twenties!) but that they're here because it seemed like the next logical step.

Some would say their parents gave them an ultimatum—school or a job—and school seemed like the better option.

And others still would declare they are in college for the parties and hot bodies on campus.

Do you want to know a secret? There is no wrong answer to that question. This stage of your life is all about figuring out who you are and what you want. It's okay to admit you don't really know where you're heading. It's even okay to admit you're mostly in this for the social opportunities.

But even if that is the case, don't you want to take full advantage of these college years? Wouldn't you rather walk away with the cool social experiences *and* the degree?

Even if you don't entirely know why you're in college or where you're heading, there is still a whole lot of good that can come from fully committing yourself to the process of learning and getting a degree—any degree. And this whole college experience? It absolutely promises to hold more value for you than you ever imagined. If only you're willing to get everything you can out of it. And in Chapter Nine, I tackle that whole question of "Why do I even need a degree or need to go to college anyway?" that eventually comes up at some point in every student's mind.

But that's the thing: You're not going to get anything out of it (besides maybe a few extra right swipes on your Tinder account) if you don't have a plan. And making that plan (a college success plan) is the first power habit of *The Study Secret*.

We all know that going to college is a big commitment, financially and otherwise. You are committing your time and these years of your life that are meant to be so formative to the process of earning a degree. And if you're like me, you're paying for most (or all) of it yourself—perhaps even taking out loans to finance that degree. That makes this decision all the more stressful.

Even if your parents are paying for everything, though, there is pressure from them and their expectations. And the responsibility to succeed is all on your shoulders.

For illustration purposes, let's focus on just the money. Let's say the next four (to six) years are going to run you a total of $50,000 in college expenses, and let's assume you need a loan for most of that. Now, if this were a business loan, no bank would lend you that money without a solid business plan in place. They know that without one, the odds of your business being a success are practically zero.

If only the same rules applied to student loans!

Unfortunately, too many students take out massive loans without fully thinking through their own plans. They assume they are borrowing this money to get a degree that will land them a job—the kind of job that will earn them a salary plenty big enough to pay off those loans. But it's not so simple, and few incoming college students have any idea what it will truly take to get to that end goal of holding their diploma. They have no plan.

Nor do they necessarily realize that even if they don't graduate, they'll still be responsible for the loans they took out in the process.

The high school system in our country is good but doesn't always offer the best prep for college in some areas. Think about it: so much of your time in high school is scheduled for you: When to go to classes, when to eat your meals, even when to study or participate in extra-curriculars. Someone was always standing behind you, telling you what to sign up for and then harping on you to remember what that schedule entailed.

Now, you're in college—and there is literally no one telling you where to be.

You are suddenly bombarded by all this newfound freedom and independence. No one tells you what to do or when to do it anymore. Sure, they give you a class schedule, but it's up to you to go—and you got to pick the times of all your classes yourself.

It's also up to you to decide when to study, when and what to eat, when or if to exercise, what other extracurricular activities to participate in, when to spend time with friends and family, and whether you should spend all day binge-watching the latest Netflix original series. This is a drastic shift from having your day-to-day life outlined for you. Now you have complete and total freedom. And while it seems amazing at first, many students become overwhelmed by it. They simply don't know what to do with their time. And when they do study, it's often with the same methods that worked for them in high school—passively paying attention and then cramming right before big exams.

> **What worked for you in high school is not going to work in college!**

That same style is not going to work for you in college.

You must adapt to the new environment and demands of college life, or you won't be successful. You absolutely need a plan—something beyond a hope or expectation in your mind to simply graduate. Without a plan, the demands ahead of you and the intense workload required to succeed will quickly drown you. The required reading alone will leave you rocking in a corner if you try to save it for the last minute. And the more you delay, the more time you'll spend trying to play catch-up, cramming all this information into days-on-end study sessions that will result in very little actually sinking in.

Remembering things for a test and actually learning them are not the same thing!

The next thing you know, your grades are dropping, you're so far behind where you want to be, and you're so exhausted that none of it seems to be working at all. Not to mention, you've had to say "no" the last few times your friends invited you out because you were so panicked about your grades. And you might be too scared or embarrassed to let your parents know what is really going on.

It's a snowball effect of failure. But you can avoid it with a solid success plan.

Which brings us to perhaps the most important question: What is a success plan?

Well, it all starts with a goal.

IDENTIFYING YOUR GOALS

There is a big difference between goals and dreams. Everyone has dreams—dreams of looking a certain way physically, having a lot of money, living in a big house, driving a really nice car, or having that ideal job or career. But I strongly believe that those dreams become goals only when you are willing to make them more specific and . . . *write them down.*

Achieving any goal is dependent on a desire for it in your heart. A weak desire is going to result in a weak effort. This means you have to have a goal you strongly desire if you're going to be motivated enough to overcome the obstacles and hardships along the way.

So what's your goal? To fulfill expectations? Is it to make your family proud? To work toward a dream career? To prove to yourself, or someone who always doubted you, that you are absolutely capable of succeeding?

Obviously, if you're here reading this book now, one goal is to graduate. But if you can pinpoint a driving force behind that goal, ideally something intrinsically motivated, you can begin the task of framing yourself within that goal.

Of making it something you actually really *want* to achieve.

Achieving a bigger, long-term goal usually involves doing something different. I mean, duh, if you do the same thing that you have always done, then it's no surprise that you're going to get the same results you always have gotten in the past. I noticed that many of my past students thought about goals kind of like winning the lottery, meaning that they were just dreams that they hoped came true someday, almost by chance. They needed a new way of thinking: Goals are achieved by taking action.

But, doing something different to achieve your goals may mean developing a new set of habits, and those changes have to come from within you. Self-motivation stems from a strong inner desire that issues in an "I can do it" attitude, even in the face of uncertainty. You're in charge of your attitude, which means only you can make up your mind (and heart) to give the pursuit of your goals 100 percent effort. If you choose to do so, then you will certainly reap the rewards of making that decision for your whole life!

Do me a favor. Put this book down for the next five minutes and contemplate what your goals are. Then, write them down in your own handwriting somewhere you won't forget.

Yes, I'm serious. Pull out a piece of notebook paper (or snag a sheet from the printer) and physically write down those goals you come up with in your own handwriting. Don't worry about whether they are long- or short-term goals for now, and don't concern yourself with trying to prioritize them just yet. Simply think about what your goals and desires are, and write them down. And it's okay to dream big and make those dreams your goals, even if they are totally unrelated to school. In fact, the more strongly you feel about them, the better. I promise, there is a point.

All set? Great! Let's talk about why I asked you to do that.

First of all, the vast majority of people don't write their goals down. So just by writing your goals down, you've already put yourself into the top tier of the population. You become a person of purpose. That is a big thing by itself. Furthermore, writing your goals down forces you to thoughtfully consider what exactly you desire and how to put it into words. Words really are powerful, so you have to choose them wisely and try to write them the way you envision your goals. Your strong desire to achieve those goals will be the fuel for your willpower to get you there.

Look back at what you wrote—did you frame your goals in a motivating light, or did you just rush to jot a few things down because I told you to? If the answer is the latter, how can you reframe what you already wrote to turn that list of goals into a powerful motivating force?

Again . . . think. Then, write.

By now you're probably wondering why I wanted you to write them in your own handwriting. Wouldn't it be easier to just type this into your laptop? Or to pull up your phone's notes app?

This is where it gets a little more complicated, but basically, when you write something down in your own handwriting, it becomes an expression of who you are. Handwriting is distinct to every individual, just like a fingerprint or voiceprint. Some piece of you is actually translated onto the paper when you write. This is why the FBI has forensic scientists who analyze handwriting and signatures, because your handwriting gives clues about who you are as a person. When you write down your goals in your own handwriting, you own them.

So turn those dreams into actual goals by always writing them down. Why? It's the crucial first step in taking your goal from a mere abstract thought to a tangible reality.

Now, you're ready for the next step: you need to keep those

goals in front of you. It does little good to write them down and then forget about them. Post them some place where you can continuously refer back to them, even speaking your goals aloud to yourself from time to time.

A vision board is simply a collage of your written goals, belief statements, positive words and related images that are displayed in a way so that you can read and be visually reminded of them daily, because of the simple fact that we tend to achieve what we focus on. If you are keeping your attention and focus on a particular goal or set of goals, then you are more likely to achieve them.

One of the best ways to do this is to create a vision board. Don't worry, your vision board doesn't need to be anything hokey that would prompt your roommate to make fun of you. It can be subtle, with pictures that remind you of your end goal and your handwritten goals displayed in a way that you can see them every day. I personally love cork boards for this, and you can decorate yours with printed statements, pictures, words, sticky notes, cut outs—pretty much whatever works for you. Let your creativity and imagination flow here. The vision board as a whole should represent what you desire and how you want to be, and its purpose is to help you get there.

Though, I should note that it is always best to keep your statements positive. So if there is anything negative that you want to change, reframe it into a positive statement. So for instance, instead of writing something like, "I will stop being such a loser on first dates," try, "I am a great listener and conversationalist on first dates!"

Okay, so maybe you wouldn't want your roommate to see that one . . . but you get the point.

For what it's worth, if you don't feel comfortable with your board being on display for all to see, you can always tuck it away in your desk or a closet—just so long as you remember to make an effort to look at it every day when you're alone. You can even take some photos of it with your smart phone, so you can always take a look when you have a free moment or feel like you may be veering off course. Consider it your life's new personalized GPS.

When you do look at your vision board, read those goals aloud occasionally and try to actively envision them. Then, make an effort to visualize your goals even when you aren't looking at that board. There are so many opportunities throughout the day to picture yourself fulfilling your goals, because the more you visualize them and keep yourself focused on them, then the more likely you are to make them a reality!

PRIORITIZING AND PLANNING

Now, let's get back to that success plan. Since you've got your goals clearly defined, I want you to pull out another sheet of paper and write at the top, "My College Success Plan."

Yes, you need to do it. Go!

Okay, now that you've got that taken care of, look over your list of goals and determine which one is your ultimate goal in relation to college. This might be the dream career, for instance, or the desire to be the first person in your family to earn a degree; basically it's the piece of the puzzle that requires you to be in college now.

Once you've determined which of your goals is your greatest priority in college, I want you to create a motivating goal statement for it and write that directly under your new "My College Success Plan" header.

You want to be as clear and specific as possible with this. For example, you might write, "I will graduate from (name of your university or college) with a bachelor's degree in (area or areas of study) by (hopeful degree year)."

Notice how this goal statement is specific to your university, your degree, your field of study and a specific graduation date. You may not be able to be that specific right now (perhaps you haven't declared a major yet), but write as much as you know or feel clear about. The important thing is to not worry or let yourself be constrained by the concept of *"how* to achieve it" just yet. For this step, you simply want to write out the end goal.

It's really easy to get overwhelmed by these big goals. Our human tendency is to think smaller than we actually want, because we don't understand *how* we could possibly achieve the real dream. But I want you to buck that tendency. In just a minute, we're going to break this goal down into more manageable chunks. But for now, I want you to remember that every amazing feat in history, from gold medal wins in the Olympics to walking on the moon, started out as just a dream.

Imagine what would have happened if Mark Zuckerberg had allowed himself to be overwhelmed by the initial idea for Facebook. He probably had no idea where it would eventually go when he first set it up. But his faith in his idea and the actions he took toward creating and following a plan transformed his vision into a platform now accessed by more than a billion active users every month.

You absolutely must make belief a part of your success plan. Believing is the indispensable factor in achieving all of your goals, no matter how big or small they may be!

Think that seems a little too high school guidance counselor-ish of me? A little too "believing is achieving" for you? Well, just for a second, imagine I made a deal with you. Let's say I were to sit you down right now and tell you that I would give you $100 for every penny that you saw on the ground and picked up during the last year. You might be able to remember a few instances where you saw a penny, but you probably didn't pick most of them up.

Now, let's say I changed the deal and told you that I was

willing to give you $100 for every penny you see on the ground and pick up over this next year. Suddenly, you're pretty excited, right? Because you believe there is a lot of money to be made with this deal—perhaps even more than you make at your current job. You imagine yourself intentionally going to populated places where there is a higher likelihood of money being dropped on the ground, easily making a few hundred dollars a day or more. Without a doubt, you would certainly find and pick up more pennies than you did in the previous year and would reap the benefits for doing so.

But let's talk about why.

Statistically speaking, the number of pennies on the ground between this year and next probably isn't going to change. We can both agree on that. But we can also probably agree that changing the dynamics of the deal will greatly affect the number of pennies you're going to find and collect. So the question becomes *why* we're so sure you'll find more, if there aren't actually more to be found?

The answer is simple: You know what you're looking for. So when the opportunity presents itself (the penny on the ground), you recognize it and pick it up, because you realize that it gets you closer to your goal (in this case, earning $100 for each penny). Plus, you believe those pennies are out there to be found.

The same is true with all your goals.

Having clearly defined and written-down goals helps you know what you are looking for. So when opportunities related to your goals present themselves, you are more likely to recognize and take advantage of them. Again, your written goals serve as a type of GPS, not only navigating you toward your destination and keeping you on the right path, but also getting you there faster. And believing in your ability to reach that end goal will improve your focus on the finish line. I personally believe that people with written goals achieve more, accomplish more, make more money, and experience more success in life.

So really, having that goal written down and believing in your ability to achieve it is half the battle.

BREAK IT DOWN

Of course it's not enough to just have the goal of graduating from college, or to believe you can do it—in this case, you need to know *how* you're going to accomplish that goal. And that involves outlining the many smaller goals that will pave the way to your eventual degree.

A few years ago, I wanted a new car. Technically, the car I had was still working fine, but it was getting up there in miles and I kept envisioning myself behind the wheel of something newer and sleeker.

Of course, I didn't exactly have the funds for something newer and sleeker, which was really the main thing holding me back.

When I was at the car wash one day, I reached down for a magazine and turned to an eye-catching ad for a gorgeous, newly designed sedan splashed across the page. It was sleek, it was beautiful, and instantly, I wanted it.

Now, keep in mind, I knew very little about the car itself at this point. I didn't know the price, or the options available, or anything about its MPG or safety features. Not to mention, all my life I had been taught that buying new instead of used when it came to cars wasn't a smart financial decision, because few things lose as much value as a car does upon being driven off the lot. And this was a brand new model, so buying used simply wasn't an option.

Still, I went home, hopped on the internet and printed off a picture of that car, adding it quickly to my first vision board. At the time, I remember somewhat doubting the effectiveness of a vision board—because seriously, how could something so simple actually work? Part of me thought I would test it out by hanging up that car picture and trying to keep myself focused on what I wanted.

After all, if a vision board was going to work in my favor, why not dream big?

The next weekend came, and I had some free time. My eyes glanced over at that picture on my vision board and I asked myself the question I'm going to ask you about your own goals here in a minute: "What's the next step to getting that car?"

I realized I needed to take some kind of action toward that goal, so I decided to take advantage of my free time and just go to the local dealership and check it out. Surely there was no harm in a test drive, right?

Getting behind the wheel only made my desire grow stronger. I loved the smooth handling, the size of the interior, the feel and smell of the leather seats and thick steering wheel, the tech features—I loved everything about it.

Unfortunately, the car was also much more expensive than I had imagined and way outside my price range.

I picked up a colorful brochure about the car before I left the dealership anyway (again, not worrying about the *how* I was going to get that car but just believing). As I thought about the whole experience, I left with more clarity about which car I wanted and the exact features I was interested in, plus an even stronger desire than I'd had before. However, I was clueless about how it was going to be possible, given the hefty price tag.

When I got home, I cut the exact color car I wanted out of the brochure, put it on my vision board and asked myself plainly, "How can I get this car?"

There was no immediate answer, but I let the question stay on my mind over the next few days.

Then it hit me. Just a few days later, I realized the next step would be to see if I could sell my current car on my own for a better price than the dealership would give me for a trade-in. I figured if I could get a certain amount for it, combined with an additional $2,000 I was expecting from an impending tax refund, I could afford the payments on the new car and stay within my budget.

I went ahead and placed an ad in the local newspaper and online to sell my car.

Within a day, I got a call from a possible buyer who showed up for a test drive and immediately offered me more cash than I had been expecting to get. That was all I needed to buy the new car. Just a few weeks after first placing that car on my vision board, I was driving it off the lot, distinctly remembering the initial experience of seeing it and falling in love, but most importantly, believing that it would actually be mine. And the only reason it was now mine was because I was clear about what I wanted and had acted on that desire.

If you are willing to do the same, then you will be surprised by how many of your goals can work out in the end. Just wait and see.

But first, you need to learn to recognize opportunity and to take action. Goals don't achieve themselves on their own; you have to have a plan and you have to take action.

So now I want you to sit down and contemplate the steps to achieving your goal. What is the next step to getting where you want to go? Is it finishing your pre-reqs? Choosing your major? Applying for internships? Finding a mentor?

Start building your college plan by breaking that big goal down into smaller, more digestible portions. And then, of course, write down those practical steps.

DECIDING ON A DEGREE PATH

Notice how I mentioned that "choosing a major" may be a part of your college success plan. That's because I fully realize not all of you will have made this decision by now, or maybe you're wavering on what you already chose. That's okay.

The truth is, the typical college student doesn't necessarily have the life experience to know what career choices are out there, which of those choices might be the best fit for them, and what type of education is necessary to enter those fields. I personally feel that we shouldn't put so much pressure on beginning college students to choose a major right away. These early years should be about exposing yourself to several possibilities, so that you can make a decision you're going to be happy with in the long run.

If you don't have a strong inclination to study a particular field, then you should simply wait. Most undergraduate degree plans have certain core courses that everyone has to take, so take those first and perhaps try an introductory course in something you find interesting. This is the best way to test the waters and start figuring out what you might want to study. I also encourage you to work in the field that interests you while you go to school, even if only on a volunteer basis or during the summer. Doing so can provide perspective on the field itself, as well as the various roles available. Seek internships, study abroad if you can, and get as much exposure as possible to different work environments, new places, languages, and cultures.

Your education is not just book- and classroom-acquired knowledge; it comes from a collection of your life experiences, too! It's all of these exciting experiences that are going to give you an appetite to pursue lifelong learning.

All that being said, the matter of changing your degree plan may come up along the way, no matter how sure you feel about your current degree path. I never thought I would change mine, but I did. And I had friends who did so multiple times during their college years. You may even decide to change colleges, too; it happens. Just beware that doing so can set you back time-wise, and a lot of money can be wasted, so don't make these decisions lightly. But don't let the time and money be the sole deterrents from doing what you truly want, either.

Under no circumstances should your college success plan be something you write out today and then never look at again. I want you to think of this as a live document—the kind of thing that is going to evolve over time. In fact, even as you read this book, I can tell you that your success plan will change. How do I know? Well, because you probably haven't included the other power habits yet, and they absolutely should be on your list of practical steps to reaching that larger goal.

Once you nail down what you want to study, you'll also want to map out your required course work as part of your college success plan. An academic advisor can help you to do this, as you work to outline what classes you'll need to graduate and in what semesters those courses are offered.

In the end, your college success plan should be a flexible map that you can continuously refer back to as you work your way toward your main goal. Without a plan, most students passively accept whatever comes their way or merely react to life's situations and challenging obstacles by always choosing the path of least resistance and developing the habit of taking the easy way out. If that's where you feel you are now, just realize that your college success plan and "can do" attitude is the remedy.

Carefully thinking through and defining your life goals (even if they change over time), coming up with a plan and taking consistent action toward it will always get you farther in life than simply coasting through it with no direction.

CHAPTER ONE ACTION STEPS

1. Start your college success plan by writing "My College Success Plan" on a piece of paper and deciding what your ultimate goal is for your education. Write this out in a clear, specific goal statement. Your plan should also include the practical steps that you are going to take to ensure your success; and don't forget to add the eight power habits presented as action statements as you work your way through this book.

2. Make a separate list of 25 to 50 goals that you desire. This list can be a mixture of short- and long-term goals that are important to you (some of which may have nothing to do with your education). These goals can serve to guide your path moving forward. Again, try and be as specific as possible.

3. Use your creativity and imagination to make a vision board. Put it in an area you visit every day so that you can see your goals and have a powerful visual reminder of what you are working toward. It can include statements, sticky notes, pictures, images, and symbols, but everything should mean something to you and help you visualize what you desire and stay focused on your goals.

2. MAKE ATTENDANCE MANDATORY

The second *Study Secret* power habit is one you're probably going to roll your eyes at initially, but I hope you'll hear me out, because it really is so important.

You need to go to class. Every day. Whether that means tuning into your e-learning lectures online, or showing up and putting your butt in a chair for your traditional classes—you need to actually be there to have any hope at all of being successful.

Between you and me, this is just common sense, right? Deep down, I have to believe you know that part of graduating college is showing up. But there is still always that allure to bailing. To playing hooky just for today . . .

The problem is that it's never just for today. And I really want you to work on quieting that voice in your head, and remind yourself that your job right now is to get that degree. And to get a degree, you have to show up.

Now, you're probably thinking I'm about to devote this entire chapter to all the token reasons you've already heard about how showing up to class allows you to build knowledge and skills progressively. You're expecting me to explain that you have to understand the fundamental concepts first, in order to build upon that foundation. Or for me to preach how going to class helps you learn discipline and how having a daily routine is great for your character and helps prepare you for "the real world." (How was that for a cliché?)

Don't even worry: I would never bore you with such obvious trivialities! I know you're smart enough to figure much of that out for yourself.

Still, recognizing the triteness of most "attendance is important" advice doesn't discount the fact that so much really is gained by the simple act of showing up.

When it comes to lecture classes, there are things you can get from the interactions between your professor and other students (not to mention between your peers themselves) that you could never replicate through borrowed notes and reading. And even with e-learning, those same interactions exist in the class chat rooms—that's why most online professors require you to log at least a few hours in there. Because actually showing up to discuss the topics helps you understand and retain the information.

Don't believe me? Think for a moment about what the brain experiences and processes when going to a theater to watch a movie, versus what is retained by just reading a short synopsis about the movie online.

Big difference, right?

Of course, your regular attendance is also crucial to your academic success for a much simpler reason: it sets the stage for you to apply most of the other power habits, reaping their benefits along the way.

Trust me, as you continue reading, you're going to see just how important showing up is.

But look, I don't want you to think that I don't get it. I know that making your own attendance mandatory isn't necessarily the easiest thing to do, especially with everything else most college students are juggling. On any given day, you're trying to prioritize your schoolwork, your job duties, your social life, and you need to sleep somewhere in there. So sometimes (maybe even a lot of the time) those other priorities can make skipping out on class seem tempting. But I want you to resist that urge. Because the benefits of attending class add up over time, lending to a little something called the compound effect.

You've probably come across this phrase before, but have you ever stopped to think about what it really means? Darren Hardy, the publisher of *Success Magazine*, defines the compound effect best in his book of the same name. Simply put, the compound effect is the principle of reaping huge rewards from a series of small, smart choices.

Basically, those daily choices add up much like compound interest, contributing to a huge payoff often beyond your wildest dreams.

Unfortunately, too many college students convince themselves skipping class is no big deal. You've probably even heard a few of your friends bragging about how they almost never go to classes but still manage to pass.

Trust me, they're not getting the same things out of their formal education as those who do attend. And even if they do still somehow pull off graduating, they're wasting a lot of valuable time and money by not taking full advantage of what attending class has to offer.

You will not only experience a better education, with lessons more likely to endure and catapult you into your career, but also have more opportunities to network with others who may just end up in the same career path as you and open up more doors to advance yours in the future.

And then, yeah, there is that real world example I promised not to mention. But seriously. Remember that college is preparing you for the working world, which requires you to be present (even if it's working remotely). That makes the habit of showing up a good one to start establishing now.

So regardless of when your classes are scheduled—make yourself go.

FOCUS ON TODAY

I hope by now I've convinced you that showing up matters. Over the next few years, you will likely spend over 1,500 hours in a classroom setting (either online or physically in that classroom space). You'll spend at least as many hours reading and studying outside of class. Plus, you have all the numerous papers, projects, quizzes and exams to look forward to.

A little overwhelming when you think of it like that, right?

So don't do that to yourself. Don't think about all the hours ahead or all the classes you have attend, all the tests, etc. Instead, just take it one day at a time.

That means committing to showing up today. Recognizing that colleges and universities break graduation goals down into smaller chunks (semesters, classes, syllabus sections) specifically because everyone understands that achieving a goal is so much easier when you focus on the smaller pieces involved in getting there.

So show up today. And while you're there, make friends with someone sitting near you. You want to get connected to your peers and start building your network. It's no secret that we all need accountability to perform our best, and knowing that someone else will notice if you're not there becomes even more motivation to show up tomorrow.

Then, ask questions. Raise your hand. Engage. Become a part of the classroom setting, not just a fly on the wall.

Because it's not just about being there. It's about actually applying yourself and actively participating when you are.

Think about it. That co-ed in your dorm with the unbelievable body, or that frat guy in your afternoon class who looks like he could bench press you—do you really think either of them got to looking the way they do by just showing up to the gym and sitting back to watch everyone else work out?

Of course not. They go, they apply themselves, and they reap the benefits.

The same is true for you. You need to apply yourself. You need to engage. You need to actively participate.

The beauty is, the more you do this, the more you'll find yourself feeling focused and alert in class and actually *wanting* to be there.

The added bonus is that your professors will begin to recognize you as a student who actually cares.

If you find yourself struggling to pay attention and engage in class though, these tips can help:

Sit Towards The Front: You are more likely to stay engaged the closer you are to the front of the classroom.

Posture: Focus on sitting up straight and leaning just slightly forward in your seat. Research shows this posture even signals to your brain to actively engage with what is being presented to you.

Distractions: Get rid of them. Put your phone in airplane mode and disable the internet on your laptop. You can always turn both back on easily as soon as class is over, but disconnecting yourself for that hour will help you pay attention now.

Preparedness: Show up to class with the book being discussed, the materials that have been assigned, and some way to take quality notes.

Get Involved: Participate in class discussions and ask questions that come to mind. If you're wondering about something, it stands to reason that someone else in the class may be, too.

If you've been struggling up to now, I can almost guarantee it's because you haven't been showing up and actively participating in your classes. All the power habits are so important, but this one is the foundation upon which they are built. So give it a try. Commit yourself to showing up and participating tomorrow. Then for the rest of the week. The rest of the month. And so on.

You have to give the compound effect time to work, and eventually, you'll be amazed at the difference it makes.

CHAPTER TWO ACTION STEPS

1. Make a definite resolution to go to class every time it meets. Show up on time. Come prepared with your completed assignments and materials to take notes. Actively participate by sitting toward the front, sitting up, leaning forward, and asking and answering questions.

2. Make friends with fellow classmates. Ask one of them to be your accountability partner, if you think you may need an extra push to stick to your commitment of showing up to every class.

3. CONNECT WITH YOUR PROFESSORS

You know that brown-noser in your first class on Mondays? The one who's always raising his or her hand, always staying after class, and forever praising whatever insights the professor has offered? Yeah . . . you're right to be annoyed by that person. Honestly, the professor is probably a bit annoyed, as well. (They can spot a suck-up a mile away).

But you know what? That suck-up is also onto something.

Look, I'm not advocating for butt-kissing. Nevertheless, taking the time to get to know your professors (and to allow them to get to know you) can go a long way toward facilitating your future success. Which is why connecting with your professors is our third *Study Secret* power habit.

The simple fact is that in any given classroom, on any given day, there is a sea of glazed faces your professor's eyes are skimming over. That sea looks very similar to the one in the class before, the day before, the semester before. And probably about 80 percent of those students will make it through the semester without ever being truly remembered by the professors handing out their grades.

But the ones the professors do remember? The faces and names that stick? Those are the students who receive the added benefits of being known—of being someone the professor actually feels connected to. Which can help in ways beyond your wildest imagination.

And which doesn't take all that much to achieve.

It starts with introducing yourself. In person.

I know, I know. For all you tech-oriented individuals, the idea of actually walking up to a professor, shaking his or her hand, striking up a conversation, and looking them in the eye as you talk might be a bit nauseating to contemplate. I get it. You want to send an email or even communicate via Snapchat. But in this one instance, for this brief moment in time, I want to encourage you to push beyond that . . . to make the effort to establish an actual human connection.

I'm going to explain *why* this is important in just a minute. But first, I want to go over *how*.

Making that initial introduction can be as simple as walking up to your professor after class and asking a relevant question. You have to introduce yourself before doing so anyway, and taking this extra step establishes you as a student who actually cares about the content of the coursework. You aren't just rushing out as soon as class is called as most do. You're staying behind, and you're coming forward with a question actually related to what was being discussed in class that day.

Of course, that requires you to pay attention enough to come up with that question. But your question doesn't even necessarily have to be about the class itself. If the professor is teaching in the field you are most interested in, you can ask about future courses he or she recommends. Or if they are serving as faculty advisor to an on-campus club you're interested in joining, you could ask about the next meeting.

Now, if other students bombard your professor after every class, or if he or she seems to be in a rush to get out of there—you may have to visit during office hours. But even that can have its benefits; doing so will often provide you with the professor's undivided attention. And going out of your way to visit during office hours can go even further to establishing you as a serious student.

Because that's really what it's all about. The benefits of making that introduction and helping your professor recognize your face and your name can be impossible to replicate any other way. By establishing this connection, you:

1. Become someone the professor is rooting for, a name they recognize when it comes time for grading.

2. Open the door for further communication, to include the request for additional help, or for an extended deadline, should you find yourself struggling later on.

3. Set the stage for this professor to become a valuable resource for you in your learning community, or perhaps a possible mentor in the future, or to be someone you could request recommendations from for an internship or higher education application.

All of these possibilities, and so many more, could serve to benefit your college success plan. But you have to make the introduction first—ideally within the first two weeks of class because that is when the best first impressions are generally made.

What about if you're taking online courses, though? Those professors are often scattered around the world and aren't necessarily available for an in-person meeting. So what do you do then?

Well, under those circumstances (and only those circumstances) leading with technology is acceptable. Shoot them an email with a similar topic starter to what you would have used for an in-person introduction. Introduce yourself and ask a question. Just make sure you do this via personal email—not during a classroom chat session.

Now, obviously, that single introduction won't guarantee the professor then knows who you are every time you interact moving forward. But it does establish the connection—one you can then nurture by participating and engaging in class. Not as the brown-noser who raises his or her hand every five minutes in an obnoxiously obvious way, but as the student who is genuinely interested, poses insightful questions, and adds to the conversation when there's something relevant to contribute.

Don't stress yourself out about trying to be teacher's pet. Just be yourself—but the version of you who isn't afraid of standing out every now and again.

GIVE A GOOD VIBE

Did you know that our brains have an automatic instinctive survival mechanism to judge whether others pose a threat to us? As a result, we consciously and subconsciously assess others in social settings based mainly on three things: their physical appearance (which includes how they're dressed), their language (and body language), and their actions.

I'm not here to tell anyone how to dress, talk or act; but I do want you to be cognizant of these things, because first impressions *do* matter. This is something we can all agree on. And making a good impression during introductions with your professors counts for a lot. So let's just go over some basics, for those who don't feel all that socially adept when engaging with their professors.

Shake hands: A firm handshake communicates confidence and respect.

Make eye contact: Resist the desire to avert your eyes, and instead hold the gaze of whomever you're speaking to. Again, this is one of the best ways to exude confidence and trustworthiness.

Distractions: For these few minutes of your day, provide your undivided attention; it's the only way you can expect anyone to give you the same.

Smile: Everyone should put on a happy face when introducing themselves for the first time. It's considered proper, courteous behavior, and it's a way to spread positivity and endear yourself to the person in front of you. Believe it or not, the first two things people notice about you are your eyes and your smile.

Some people will have an easier time making these introductions than others. I recognize that for the introverts among us, it can be hard to put yourself out there like this. But it's so important, and one of those life skills that will serve you long beyond college, because these skills are good in any formal setting, including job interviews. So try. Push yourself. And remember, it's only a few minutes that can make a big difference in your college experience.

THE NEXT STEPS

Let's be honest: Establishing yourself as a name and face your professor knows increases your chance of being called on in class. Which can be a bit intimidating for a lot of people, even if you feel like you understand the material pretty well. There is just something about having all eyes on you—especially when you didn't volunteer to answer a question—that can create a little stress.

But *don't* stress. Even if you don't know the answer, the worst thing that can happen is you respond with, "I'm sorry, Professor. I don't really know. I actually had questions about that topic myself and wanted to ask if you could clarify it a bit more." With an answer like this, you've communicated in a mature way that you're not sure—but that you care about learning more.

Of course, by practicing the eight power habits that you are now learning in this book, you'll be plenty prepared to answer any questions that come your way!

THE KEY TO GETTING WHAT YOU WANT

Now, let's talk about one of the most obvious (and short-term) benefits of making these introductions: Establishing this connection early on makes it easier for you to ask for help later. Because . . . duh. Introducing yourself when you *don't* need something is a heck of a lot more genuine than waiting until you do.

Life happens. We get sick, experience family emergencies, get in car accidents, lose loved ones, or hit major conflicts in our schedules at the most inopportune times. I will preach showing up to class and applying yourself all day long—but even I recognize that, sometimes, life gets in the way.

We've all had to reach out to a teacher or professor at some point in time to ask for something. Whether it's requesting PowerPoint slides from a missed class or the leeway to turn in a paper late, there will come a point when you need something from at least one of your professors. And you're a whole lot more likely to receive a positive response if you're someone who has previously established a connection with that professor.

Now, I am going to give you a word of warning: College professors are highly trained human lie detectors. They've heard every story in the book, and they can see through whatever "creative nonsense" you might be thinking of throwing their way. So don't ever put that connection you have worked to build in jeopardy by fabricating excuses or trying to get out of something you are perfectly capable of doing. The advice I'm about to give you is really and truly only for when those life moments hit that you have no other way around.

Abuse these tips, and you'll establish yourself as a flake, not as the truly dedicated student you want your professors to perceive you as being.

Okay, now that we've got that word of warning out of the way, how *are* you supposed to react when those derailing life moments hit? Or when you find yourself struggling in a class you really have been trying your best in?

Many young people find it incredibly difficult to ask for help effectively and still keep their developing or newfound adulthood about them. There's danger of slipping into that high-pitched, strained, excuse-making voice kids often use when they're confronted with an authority figure. In fact, many young college students are still oblivious to using that voice because it's all they know.

But when you hit those latter high school years and early adulthood, the social rules and expectations change regarding what kind of voice you use.

The *only* option is to start embracing a mature mindset, which is expressed through the mature voice that comes with adulthood (at least for most people). The mature mindset is what people are referring to when they tell others to "grow up" or "stop being immature." It's the mindset that your parents, teachers, coaches, mentors, employers (and future employers), boyfriend or girlfriend, and even society at large are all hoping develops in you as you enter adulthood.

The mature mindset recognizes, respects and follows:

authority	heirarchy	responsibilities
rules	structure	common sense
laws	schedules	common courtesy
instructions	timelines	polite manners
order	deadlines	social norms

The mature mindset is objective and recognizes why we need all of these things in order to have a productive society and quality life. Think about it, without them, society would be total chaos. The mature mindset does not always necessarily agree with all of these principles all of the time, but it knows how to disagree appropriately without challenging or threatening authority.

Most importantly, the mature mindset accepts responsibility and is willing to take all necessary measures to fulfill an obligation, keep a promise, and right a wrong, even if it means inconvenience and extra work.

Read that last sentence again. It's so important.

You need to learn how to use the mature voice to ask for help. What is the mature voice? Well, it's the voice that errs in the exact opposite direction of where your instincts might tell you to go.

Don't take that the wrong way. We all have a bit of immaturity begging to get out when we feel ourselves backed into a corner. Our immature voice implores us to whine, to place blame, to victimize ourselves and pull out the puppy dog eyes and plead. The immature voice is excellent at using language to *manipulate*.

But our mature voice knows better. It uses language to *negotiate*. And sooner or later you're going to realize that you mostly get out of life what you negotiate, which is even more reason to embrace the mature mindset and master the mature voice. It's the voice that understands most professors will respond far more positively to honesty and cool heads than to "It wasn't my fault!" and "I'm a victim!"

That type of stuff may have worked on your parents your entire life and maybe some of your high school teachers let it slide, but your professors aren't interested. I can promise you that.

So whatever it is you find yourself needing, I want you to school yourself in the mature voice before approaching your professors. Remember that the mature voice accepts responsibility and recognizes the importance of deadlines, even when the problem is that those deadlines can't be met. The mature voice doesn't threaten or beg; it accepts responsibility, presents the facts and humbly requests assistance.

Let me illustrate with a true story: I missed a deadline for turning in an important paper because I honestly forgot when it was due (I know—super lame excuse). I told the professor that I understood and absolutely agreed with the reason for the deadline on the paper (letting them know that I had a mature mindset) and that I did not have a reason for missing it other than that I simply forgot the due date. (I was honest.) But here is the kicker . . . I then told the professor that I really wanted to learn the material related to the paper and that I would voluntarily write an even longer paper than initially assigned. I would still turn it in for their feedback, even if I wasn't going to get any points. In this case, the professor was impressed with my sincere desire to learn and ended up giving me credit for it.

Even though it wasn't necessary in this instance, the mature voice also graciously accepts defeat. Because no matter how maturely you ask, your professors may not always be able to accommodate your needs. Blowing up and losing your cool when that happens won't help your case. But responding with, "I understand. Thank you for hearing me out" just might.

Even if you don't agree, respond maturely. Your professors need to see you are someone who can deal with disappointment like an adult. In an instance where they don't come around to your side at the end of an initial discussion, leave the door open with something like, "Well, I disagree with your decision and hope that you might reconsider and change your mind. Let me know if you do."

But between you and me—we've all known plenty of grown adults who still struggle with responding to any given situation maturely. Which is perhaps why it is all the more impressive when a college student can pull this off; it's not expected and it sets you apart.

So no matter how unlikely what you are requesting may be (for instance, recognize that most professors have policies about makeup exams and project deadlines), it never hurts to ask. And even if you're turned down, a mature reaction on your part, and a willingness to accept responsibility for the role you played in getting to where you now are, may just leave your professor wanting to find another way to help you.

Need an example of how one of these conversations might go? Well, let's say you bombed the last exam. A mature response would be to go to your professor's office and lead the conversation with, "I know I didn't study enough for this exam. I attended every class and spent three hours preparing for it, but I should have done more. I really want to get a better grade on this next one. Can you give me any advice on how to better prepare for it?"

You've done a couple things here. You've taken responsibility, you've let your professor know you are disappointed in your own performance, and you've shown initiative in wanting to do better in the future. Most professors will respond kindly to this type of approach, especially since you have been putting forth effort. Some may even help you with study guides or give you the opportunity to turn in an extra assignment to boost your grade.

These are the kinds of opportunities you never would have had if you hadn't bothered to ask.

They're the kinds of opportunities that may not have been available to you at all if you were just another face in the crowd.

So take the steps to get connected with your professors. Make the introduction. And then work to nurture that connection and to approach your professor maturely when you need something down the line.

I promise, there are no better advocates to have in the pursuit of your college and post-graduate degrees.

CHAPTER THREE ACTION STEPS

1. Take definite steps to meet each professor within the first week or two of class. If they are not available after class or when you arrive at office hours, leave a handwritten note letting them know you came by to meet them.

2. Make positive first impressions with firm handshakes, eye contact, and genuine smiles.

3. Embrace the mature mindset and practice using the mature voice.

4. SMART SCHEDULING

So by now you realize just how crucial having a plan is to succeeding in school—and in life, for that matter. If you don't know what you're working toward and how you're going to get there, you're never going to accomplish your goals, right?

Well, the same concept applies to scheduling your time—and that is the next power habit we're going to discuss. Was there ever a point in high school when you realized you just couldn't do it all? Maybe you wanted to play on a sports team, participate in a few school clubs, get good grades (so that you could get into college!) and still have time for a job—and your friends. You probably realized at some point that something had to give—not only did you have scheduling conflicts (like the yearbook staff meeting at the same time as soccer practice), but you also found yourself struggling to find time for schoolwork.

The result? You had to make some choices. And then you had to start thinking about how to arrange your own schedule.

The thing is, in high school, most of us still had some help with this. Your parents were probably there giving you reminders, you were doing a lot of activities your friends were also participating in (so you had their motivation to count on), and the school probably gave you some leeway and guidance, as well.

Now you're in college. Scheduling your life is pretty much all up to you. Which is kind of awesome and kind of terrifying at the same time.

I had a mentor once upon a time who used to say, "**What gets scheduled is what gets done.**" I know it sounds a little nerdy, but I know it's true! I've done it both ways, and I can tell you firsthand: Scheduling is absolutely a key to success.

Without a schedule, it's so easy to procrastinate. Of course you would rather go to that party with your friends or hit up the beach on a weekend! If the choice is between that or studying, who wouldn't choose the social time? But the thing is, with a solid schedule—you can probably do both.

Think about it. Remember earlier in the week when you were just sitting around scrolling through your Twitter feed and watching YouTube videos for two hours? If you had scheduled that time to finish your paper up instead, you might not have found yourself needing to do that work on the weekend—you could have avoided procrastinating and bought yourself some valuable social time in the process.

But scheduling your time is only partly what saves you from wasting time on unproductive activities.

THE CURE FOR PROCRASTINATION

I'm not a psychologist but after considering my own experience and working with hundreds of students as an educator, I think most people view procrastination as a time-management problem.

But I don't think it is.

I believe procrastination is more of an emotion-management problem related to self-gratification. Simply put, we want what makes us feel good *right now* (even if that's doing nothing), so we tend to put off doing any activities that are less enjoyable.

Translation — we wait until the last day, last hour, even last minute to take care of important tasks and meet deadlines.

By this time, we are usually in an emotional tornado of stress, panic, frustration, and perhaps self-condemnation for having waited to do everything. And it goes without saying that this isn't the best state of mind to cram for that big test, write that paper or finish up that project due in less than 24 hours. If you're smiling right now, it's because you know I'm right.

So, what is the cure for procrastination?

First, you have to realize the cure is not a "once-for-all" kind of cure. Nope, our tendency to procrastinate never goes away because it's our human nature. Think of it like a screensaver program that just comes on automatically after a period of inactivity. And it just takes one small step to get rid of that screensaver—a simple click of any key.

That's the same cure for procrastination. No, not a key stroke— but taking a small step.

Breaking any task into smaller steps and taking action on that first one, regardless of how you feel, is the cure to every bout of procrastination.

Because procrastination is fundamentally an emotional issue, you don't have to wait on your emotional state to organically reach some certain place before you can start working on whatever task is in front of you. In other words, you don't have to feel like doing something to actually do it. You pull a Nike and just do it.

The focus is not on how you *feel* but on *taking action*. Taking that first small step and getting started is the key.

As a student, I learned that the more I dreaded something, the smaller the steps I needed to mentally break that task down into, even to the point of almost being ridiculous (what I called "the baby steps"). For example, if I needed to research and write a long paper, then I would even get it down to 1) Stand up. 2) Walk over to the computer. 3) Turn on the computer . . . And inwardly, I would ask myself, "Can you stand up and walk over to the computer?" And knowing how easy those baby steps were, then I would take action and get started.

It was as if taking action on those small steps gave me just the momentum and lift I needed to get above all the clouds of my emotion. So I taught this same strategy to my students with a lot of success.

I continue to use it today. Trust me, this is a mental coping strategy that will help you for the rest of your life.

As reinforcement, I still use the activities I would rather do (tweeting, surfing the web, gaming, going out with friends or family, etc.) as little rewards to myself for getting the important stuff done.

Now we are ready to see how pairing this "small step strategy" (and temporarily delaying our gratification) with the power habit of smart scheduling your time will make you the most productive.

MAKE A WEEKLY PLANNER

First, it's always a good idea to create a visual representation of your time. Otherwise, it's so easy to convince yourself you have time for everything or time for nothing. Actually mapping it out and creating something you can look at allows you to see when that may be true, and when something has to give.

You don't have to rush out and buy a fancy planner, though. Most smartphones have calendar apps you can use for your schedule. Or you could easily print off a weekly planner sheet from the internet. You could even draw one yourself on a sheet of paper.

It doesn't really matter what you use, just so long as it allows you to physically see how your blocks of time are being spent.

Next, I want you to spend some time scheduling everything you know you must do in a day. And I mean, everything. Schedule your sleep, your meal times, your exercise routine, and even the travel to and from class. Block out when you'll be in your lectures, when you have to be at work, and any other routine commitments you keep— like church or sports. Basically, anything you know you have to do belongs on this schedule.

You should be looking at a pretty solidly booked week, since you're scheduling everything. But there will still be blocks of time when you don't have anything planned, and there will certainly be things you need to do that didn't necessarily make the list. Grocery shopping, laundry and routine cleaning, for instance, are the kinds of errands and chores that sometimes don't come up until you actually need to do them. That's okay . . . though, I would suggest trying to schedule those things for the weekends, when you don't have as much else going on. And honestly, if you make a habit of scheduling them, you might find you're able to stay on top of these chores and errands better than ever before.

Translation: you won't run out of clean underwear anymore.

Of course, you want to schedule social activities, as well. No one can survive on study and work alone. And after all the studying you'll be doing, you'll deserve a break as a reward for all that hard work!

Now that you have everything on a schedule, I want you to sit back and look at it . . . really look at it. Where are your open blocks of time? When in your day and week do you have nothing scheduled at all?

Get ready: That's when you'll be studying.

Start by looking for the biggest blocks of time, those that are one hour or longer. In order to smart schedule your time, you also must consider *where* you will be during your day, because sometimes we don't realize how much time we waste traveling between activities. So, plan ahead and label where you'll be right before and after those big open blocks to maximize your time.

For instance, you might finish a class on campus at 10 a.m. and not have to be at work off campus until 1 p.m. Seeing that chunk of time and knowing where you need to be for each of those scheduled items might trigger the realization that you would be better off heading to the library to study after your class than trying to make the 15-minute trek home. That time you would have spent traveling from campus to your apartment or dorm, and then from there to work, could instead be spent doing your required reading. Afterward, you could grab lunch on campus (thereby saving even more time) before heading straight to work from there.

Other examples that helped me smart schedule were bringing my work clothes to campus and changing there, instead of going back home and losing more travel time. I also used to drive to work or school early to avoid high traffic times and then stay in my car in the parking lot to study until it was time to start my shift or class. Or to save both money and time, I would sometimes bring leftovers from dinner to eat for lunch on campus or in my car rather than having to go find something. These were all little changes in my routine that added up to big gains.

PLAN OUT WHERE YOU CAN READ AND STUDY

Where you study is just as important as when you study. Obviously, if you're trying to study in the middle of campus, as your peers walk all around and your friends stop to say "hi" every five minutes, the constant distractions are going to keep you from getting any kind of quality work done. It won't matter if you have three hours to dedicate to studying, because with all those interruptions, you would have been better off cutting your study time in half and heading home to at least do your work in peace.

Our brains need quiet and the absence of distraction for effective studying to take place. And when I'm talking about distractions, I'm not just talking about your friends and family; I'm also talking about your phone.

How many times have you sat down to study, gotten in the zone, and then been interrupted by a text message? Notifications for this or that? You pick your phone up "real quick," telling yourself it will "just take a second." But then, before you know it, you've spent an hour scrolling through Facebook, texting with a friend, checking out that crazy gif and reading the latest celebrity gossip.

Our constant state of connectivity is the worst possible thing for productivity.

My advice?

Get Out Of The Dorm: I loved dorm life, and I would absolutely recommend every college student give living in the dorms a try. But when it comes to studying, go anywhere but the dorms. There is just always something going on, and there are always people looking to hang out or coerce you away from your books. Dorms are a great place to sleep, socialize, and make life-long friends. They aren't the best place to study. And even if you live in an off-campus apartment, consider dedicating a space that isn't your room to studying. Most of our rooms are jam-packed with distractions—you'd be better off establishing a nook in your living room as your go-to study spot. Try a space that's preferably out of sight of your television and video game consoles, because you don't even need to see those distractions while you're trying to focus.

Turn Your Phone Off: I know, I know . . . It can feel like torture to disconnect yourself. But imagine watching a movie you really like, except every few minutes you leave the room and then return to continue watching. Are you going to understand the movie? Probably so, but it's going to be disjointed in your mind as you're missing parts. Your brain actually needs to focus on a single task in order to optimize learning. Multitasking with your phone, or toggling back and forth with other media while you are studying is detrimental to the learning process. Eliminating distractions will improve the quality and efficiency of this time, so that it takes you three hours to do what it might have taken you five with all the distractions.

Disable Your Internet: For all the same reasons as above, if you need to study with your laptop, do so with the internet off. Or, if you need to use the internet for your studying, consider downloading one of those apps that will prevent you from logging into certain social networking sites during specific hours. The technology to do so exists specifically because so many people have come to realize just how distracting those sites can be . . . and sometimes, you just need to cut yourself off completely to be able to focus.

The library is usually a great place to study on campus, but scope out a few backup spots as well—libraries tend to fill up during certain hours, and especially as midterms and finals approach. There may be unoccupied classrooms or study niches across campus that you can turn to when you need a quiet and distraction-free zone.

THE LITTLE BLOCKS OF TIME MAKE THE DIFFERENCE

Those big blocks of time are great for working on assignments or really focusing in on what you need to study. But you may have noticed your schedule is also full of small, uncommitted blocks of time. Fifteen minutes between classes here, 30 minutes to spare there—these little segments can actually be the key to getting ahead in your study goals. They're another key component in smart scheduling your time.

But how much studying can you really get done in a spare 10 minutes? Well . . . more than you might think. I'm telling you, the small blocks of time are going to be your secret weapon to help you get ahead (or catch up)! Especially when you pay attention to just how quickly those small chunks of time add up.

Don't believe me? Take a highlighter to all those little chunks laid out in your schedule for the week ahead. Then whip out your calculator and add the time up.

Pretty impressive, right? Little things add up to big things.

It can be really easy to grasp onto these smaller blocks of time as opportunities to review your last class' notes, study for an upcoming quiz, learn new vocabulary, or work on anything you have to memorize.

Or use them to start the first small steps of a bigger task. For example, you may have an upcoming paper to write, so use 20 minutes to find some good quality sources on the internet now. Later, you can read them in-depth and finally write that paper. Or perhaps you have to read an entire book for your English Lit class within five days; you should be able to easily finish at least one chapter.

Let's say that in the week ahead, you have about 15 hours of studying and completing assignments to factor in. If you were to wait just for your hour or longer blocks of time to get to work, you would probably find yourself wasting your weekend away finishing it all up. But by smart scheduling some of those smaller blocks of time, you might be able to shave an hour or more off that total study commitment each and every day—which buys you at least an additional five hours for socializing this weekend—yahoo!

Let's be real, you weren't doing anything worthwhile with those smaller time blocks anyway. No one utilizes them consistently, which is why they are going to help you catch up, stay on track and ultimately, get ahead. So using them to your advantage and shaving time off your total study commitment is just smart scheduling!

CHAPTER FOUR ACTION STEPS

1. Establish a weekly planner, either on your phone or on a piece of paper, that allows you to map out the entire week in blocks of time.

2. Label and mark off the time you spend sleeping, getting ready, eating, exercising and traveling.

3. Label and mark off your class schedule and work schedule, and make note of where you will be before and after each activity so that you can minimize travel and down time and maximize study time.

4. Find the remaining blocks of time and mark out the one-hour blocks and longer for study time.

5. Highlight the blocks shorter than one-hour long, adding them up to see how taking advantage of those smaller blocks could shave time off your total study commitment.

5. POWER READING

You've probably noticed by now that practically every single one of your college professors harps on the importance of the reading. You sit down on that first day of class, and they all greet you with a foreboding message about just how much reading you'll have to do in order to be successful in their class.

If you're like most college students, you probably rolled your eyes at those warnings at first.

I'm guessing you're not rolling your eyes anymore.

The reason all your professors push that reading is because, unlike high school teachers, they have no intention of spoon-feeding you the knowledge you need. Remember, your college professors certainly want you to succeed, but they're under no obligation or pressure to *make* you succeed. It's not their civic responsibility to make sure you test well. That ended with your high school diploma.

They expect you to read prior to classes so that they can hit the ground running, diving deeper into the concepts their lecture intends to explore without having to waste time on the basics.

That's why they really do expect you to do the reading to keep up.

And it's also why power reading is our next *Study Secret* power habit.

Now, for the record, I totally get how daunting all that reading can be. I mean, do they really expect you to read that many pages a week? And don't they know all your other professors are asking the same? If you're a person who sometimes struggles to read anything longer than text messages and emails, then digesting all of those textbooks can seem nearly impossible.

Deep breaths . . . I'm going to show you how to tackle that reading the right way. Because it really is possible to do it all. I promise.

Why do you have to do the reading, though? Or why can't you just skip out on buying the textbooks (which, let's be honest, are crazy expensive) and share with someone else instead?

Listen, I'm not going to sugarcoat this for you. There is no easy way out here. You have to do the reading, because you won't have the fundamental building blocks to succeed in your courses if you don't. To be brutally honest: You will not get a good education if you choose not to do all the reading.

Yes, you have to buy the textbooks, because you need to get in the habit of writing in them, highlighting important sections, and making notes as you go—something that, I promise, will actually save you heaps of time in the long run. Because if you study right the first time around, notating your reading as you go, you won't be caught in panic mode ever again.

Forget any hope of keeping those books in pristine condition so that you can sell them back to the bookstore. If you market them right, you might actually be able to get more money by selling them yourself after the fact; just think about how helpful your notes and highlighting will be to the next student who gets your books! This is what I did.

GET IN A STUDY STATE OF MIND

First things first: You need to really map out how much reading you have to do, and by when. Taking the time to do that up front is the best way to not only ensure all your reading gets done, but that you're not in panic or cramming mode trying to read 200 pages the night before a class—a habit that won't have you retaining much of the information anyway.

Start by tracking all your reading assignments, from all your classes, on one notebook page or snap pics of the schedules so that you always have them with you. Most of your professors will have already done you the favor of assigning your reading in digestible chunks, so you just need to have a schedule of when all that reading is due in your own a single reference place.

Now that you've got it all written out in chronological order, count the number of pages due prior to the deadline days, and then divide the total number of pages by the number of days available to get the reading done. This will help you to determine how many pages for each class you should be reading a day. Let's face it: Having to read 30 pages a day sounds better than having to read over 200!

Again, we are taking a bigger task and breaking it down into smaller portions. I call this "pacing your reading," and with more practice, you will be able to accurately estimate how much time you need to finish reading assignments. This idea is especially important since you are going to be reading a little differently than you're used to, because I'm going to teach you to power read.

Once you've calculated your daily reading responsibility, be sure to include the time for that reading on your schedule. Because getting behind on your reading is the last thing you want to do—that's how you wind up either missing out on the reading that needs to be done, or subsisting on coffee as you try to do it all in one session (which, again, obviously isn't that great for retention.)

But then there's the matter of *how* you read.

I know, I know . . . you're rolling your eyes again. Because you've been doing this whole reading thing for quite a while, right? You know how to translate those letters on a page into meaningful content in your head.

Except, maybe you haven't been doing it in the way your brain most likes to learn.

Sure, you know how to look at words on a page and decipher what they're saying. But as you may have already discovered, trying to read big chunks of information in one sitting can sometimes leave you cross-eyed, or suddenly realizing it's been 15 minutes or 10 pages since you actually retained a single idea. Don't feel bad . . . it happens to the best of us. But it's also exactly why you need to make sure your brain is ready before you ever start to read.

How you read is just as important as where you read (ideally a quiet, distraction-free zone). And if you take the time to do the power reading right the first time, you won't find yourself struggling to pour over the same material again and again as you try to digest the concepts later.

So before you ever start to study or read, make sure your brain is ready. That's right—to maximize learning, you need to properly prep your brain first. Look, your brain needs energy to function, hydration to operate efficiently, and a reduction of stress to focus and process new information in a meaningful way. Having as few distractions as possible will further help you concentrate on what you're learning from the reading.

Here are some tips for keeping your brain in tip-top shape at the start of, and throughout, your study sessions:

Get enough sleep. If you're exhausted, you won't be able to focus. Listen to your body, but most late teens and young adults need eight hours or more of sleep each night.

Keep nuts and fresh or dried fruits and veggies The kind of things you can easily grab to snack on, and the type of snack that is especially beneficial for studying; whole foods with brain-boosting nutrition.

Do some deep breathing exercises whenever you're feeling stressed. Or schedule in time for a run to boost your endorphins. Or spend some time focusing on your goals, your vision board, and what you hope to achieve. The body's fight or flight response is intense, and incredibly distracting, so if you're overly stressed or anxious, then your mind is not in learning mode. Finding ways that work for you to keep the stress at bay is one of the best things you can do for your study success.

POSITIVE SELF-TALK

Another super important tip—and one of the most effective ways to deal with fears, doubts, stress and anxiety—is to regularly engage in positive self-talk.

Remember Dory, from *Finding Nemo and Finding Dory*? "Just keep swimming, just keep swimming..." Do you know why she repeated that to herself again and again? It was because she was scared of the ever deepening, dark water she found herself swimming through. To take her mind off that fear and to motivate herself to go on, she sang that little phrase to herself.

That's positive self-talk. And we all talk to ourselves inside our head at times.

I know it might sound weird, but it is a powerful tool to not only de-stress and deal with anxieties and doubts that often creep into our minds, but also to keep ourselves motivated.

Of course, you don't have to sing to yourself, unless you want to.

Need some ideas for how to make positive self-talk work for you? Well, you might tell yourself, "You are a hard worker, and you can do this." Or, if you're in the middle of a long reading passage, "Just keep reading! Just keep reading!"

Of course, many of us are predisposed to negative self-talk, because we often think negatively without realizing it. Or as the case was with many of my students, they were raised in an environment filled with negative talk that really hindered them without their realization. They were quick to go to a place of "I can't do this" or "This is too hard" or "I'm not smart enough." However, as a rule I didn't allow any negativity in my classroom but maintained a very positive atmosphere in which I daily modeled positive self-talk.

Not only so, I made sure that every student knew that I believed in them as a person and in their ability to succeed. To this day, I still feel that this was perhaps my best contribution to my students' lives, because how you talk to yourself is a reflection of how you think, and how you think is a reflection of who you are.

You need to pay attention to how you talk to yourself, because that negative self-talk has just as much power to push you down as the positive self-talk has to build you up.

Make positive self-talk one of your new goals, and put it on your vision board. Positive self-talk spawns positive outcomes, but negative self-talk spawns negative outcomes. You *can* change the way you talk to yourself. Like everything else, it just takes some focus and effort to get there.

POWER READING PREP

Now that your brain is calmer and ready to focus on the reading, there are a few other things you should be doing before you really dive in—because power reading isn't just about glossing over those words on the page. It's about actually being able to digest what you see. Before you start to read any new chapter, you need to first scope out the content and see how much material you have ahead of you and what you can expect to cover. Think of this step as prepping your brain as a blank canvas before you start painting on it with all the information that your power reading and studying. You're basically setting the stage for optimal learning, so don't skip it.

Start by flipping through the pages and reading all the chapter titles, headings, and subheadings. And pay attention to any boldface and highlighted words; these usually indicate new vocab. being introduced.

You may also come across some comprehension questions

throughout the text. Read those carefully; they can help guide you in where to pay most attention as you begin reading the chapter more comprehensively.

Know that you probably won't understand most of what you're seeing just yet. That's okay. This prep is more about providing your brain with the framework of what's to come. It's like spreading out all the puzzle pieces for your brain to make the big picture.Again, this power reading prep is crucial to stimulate and engage your brain to maximize learning, so if you're not used to it, it may feel a little awkward at first or like you're wasting time, but you're actually doing your brain a big favor.

THE "WHY" BEHIND WHAT YOU DO WHILE YOU READ

Understanding how your brain works through and learns new information really helps you get the most out of reading. During my teacher training, I was taught that it's best to present new concepts to students by using real objects or hands-on experiences first, because these things are easily understood and processed by our brains.

Next, you take these concepts and make representations of them using pictures, drawings or other images that represent the objects and your real-life interactions with them. Lastly, you add the labels, symbols and words that define, describe and explain these concepts on an abstract level.

So you start with the concrete, real-life objects and actions, then make a representation of those same things, and finally use words or symbols to explain all of this at the advanced abstract level.

A quick elementary example of this could be me teaching you the concept of addition. I start with real-life objects and I give you 10 marbles to hold and count. Then, I give you five more marbles and ask how many you have now altogether. You physically count each one and tell me 15.

Now, we move to representing what we just did. So I ask you to draw 10 marbles on a piece of paper that represent the 10 marbles you started out with and to draw a circle around that group of 10 marbles. You then draw a second group of five marbles and draw a circle around that group, which represents the additional ones I gave you. You follow this step by drawing a new group of 15 marbles and putting a circle around them.

Now come the abstract labels and symbols. Lastly, I ask you to write out the numerical symbol "10" by your circled group of 10 marbles, and "5" and "15" by their respective circled groups. I further explain that we use the symbol "+" to indicate addition and what the "=" symbol means. To conclude the whole process, we write out 10 + 5 = 15 with the sentence "Ten marbles plus five marbles equals fifteen marbles," as a completely abstract expression of everything we just did.

This process of moving from the concrete to representations and then to the abstract is the way our brain learns best in the beginning. However, the problem is that as we advance from elementary school through high school and into college, less time and attention is given to the real-life, hands-on experiences and the more the teaching is done purely at the abstract level.

Remember, words are abstract, and all of your reading is in words (more specifically formal book language, which even differs from how we speak in everyday life). This is why it's important to visualize what you're reading as it unfolds in the book, making representations of it in your head. Visualizing these representations not only helps you make connections and understand the material but also remember it.

That's easier to do with fiction, but most of what you read in college textbooks is nonfiction. For this reason, it's important to interact with your abstract reading material and work backwards. This way, it's almost like you're translating the abstract content you're reading back into representations that indicate the important unseen connections that you are making in your mind.

So power reading has nothing to do with how fast you read, and it differs from just regular reading because of the pre-reading prep and, more importantly, what you do to process the abstract information while you're reading.

In order to power read you will need to always have a highlighter and pen with you. With the highlighter, you should mark all the new definitions, important concepts, and key terms or repeated phrases. With the pen, you're going to make brief notes, formulate questions or thoughts, draw arrows to show connections or relationships, add symbols, create acronyms and even small drawings in the margins to emphasize anything in the text that stands out to you. All of these notes will serve as little mnemonic devices, or memory aides, that act as retention cues for your brain.

In my experience, it's really common for students to struggle with deciding what's most important from the material they're presented with, which often translates into students trying to write too much and over-process the text, or highlight too lengthy of sections.

Don't do that.

The following list is meant to help you create a framework for what's most important in a college text:

Learning new definitions or specialized terminology

Identifying the main idea of the content

Knowing the what, how, and why of a given topic

Recognizing cause and effect relationships

Recognizing the order of events

Comparing and contrasting two or more things

Understanding and applying the steps to a process or formula

Understanding relationships between topics discussed

Analyzing and synthesizing data

Drawing logical conclusions

Making practical applications to the real world

Making judgments or giving opinions and supporting them with your ideas or facts

I have further broken these down into the three broad categories and a handy little acronym just to help your brain remember—V.I.P. (V=Vocabulary, I=Ideas and Concepts, P=Patterns and Relationships).

When you come across anything within these categories in your reading, you can use a type of shorthand to take notes in the margins. For instance, C/E for "cause and effect" or MI for "main idea." You can even use symbols such as a mini-Venn Diagram to indicate "compare and contrast" or other symbols such as asterisks or stars and little pictures or drawings, all of which aid the brain in understanding and recall.

In this way, not only are you drawing attention back to the most important facts when you engage in a review later, but you're also setting your brain up to instantly recall how that piece of text relates back to the main subject at hand. And if, as you're reading, you come across a subject that was discussed in a previous lecture class, make sure to make a note of that. What professors emphasize from the reading in their lectures has a very good chance of ending up on a quiz or test.

All these notes, little drawings, arrows, and highlighted words you're making as you read serve as retention cues and mile markers for your brain. What you write and what system you personally use are not that important, as long as whatever you do makes good sense to you and you're consistent with your method. It may feel really weird for you to do this in the beginning, but with experience and practice you will easily find a system that works for you and begin to do it automatically with quickness and ease. Just keep at it.

Now, if you find yourself reading and struggling to process the text (one of those moments where you realize you haven't retained any of it,) try going back and re-reading just that section aloud. This can help your brain to refocus and connect to the material in front of you.

Then again, if you've just been reading for too long and you can't connect to that material at all . . . take a brain break. In fact, you should be scheduling these brain breaks into your study time. Allow yourself a five-minute break to disengage from the material every 30 to 45 minutes or so. Stand up, walk around, and get a snack—with time you will build up your reading stamina.

Some people find that taking a brief nap can help them get back on track if their mind starts to wander or they begin losing focus. In fact, research shows that taking a short nap (around 15 minutes) can reenergize you and recharge your brain. The secret is not to nap too long though, or you risk waking up even groggier than you were before the nap, because you throw off your body's natural rhythm.

For the record, this doesn't work for everyone—plenty of people can't pull off the short nap. And that's okay. Experiment with it a little. If it helps, great! If not, and you find yourself losing study hours and struggling to sleep at night, nix the naps and focus on getting at least eight hours of rest every night.

MAKING CONNECTIONS = LEARNING

As you power read, you should always actively think about what the "big-picture idea" is and how all the information is related to it. Pose this question to your mind and even see your reading as the unfolding of that answer. Nearly all books and lectures are organized in such a manner to always have a "big-picture idea" in the same way that all the puzzle pieces of a jigsaw puzzle eventually make a big picture.

So, as you're reading, the most important thing you can do is make a concerted effort to connect together the concepts you're learning about. It's not enough to just know the vocabulary, or the dates of events or the basics behind certain theories; you have to know how it all weaves together.

Making those connections is learning, and it is the connections you make that also help you to retain the information for the long term.

For this reason, I want you to really stop and focus every time you come across any comprehension questions in your text. Remember, you should have already read them once in your pre-reading prep. But now, I want you to really consider them. These questions are specifically designed to help you test your comprehension of the material as a whole—to piece together how it all connects. Think of them as clues to what is important in the reading, and it's likely that professors may use some of these for any pop quizzes.

If you can't answer one of these questions for any reason, it's time to go back through the material and figure out what you might be missing. Don't move forward until you feel as though you have a solid grasp of what you've already covered. And consider highlighting those questions and making a note of what page the answers can be found on for your future review—you'll save yourself time when studying for midterms and final exams later! It's easy to make trying to finish the reading more important than making sure you understand it.

If there is anything you truly just don't get, then be sure and bring it up in class or in your study group. Your professors want you to engage with the reading, and chances are if you are struggling with something, others are, too. It's perfectly normal to not understand everything, but seek out that understanding. That's what getting a good education is all about.

CHAPTER FIVE ACTION STEPS

1. Always purchase the required textbooks for your assigned classes.

2. Always have a pen and highlighter with you as you read so that you can process the text.

3. Learn to recognize what's important and make notes, highlight, and make representations about any important ideas and concepts in the reading.

4. Use any comprehension questions as clues to what is important to understand in the reading material.

6. HACK YOUR NOTES

In case you haven't figured it out yet, a big part of *The Study Secret* is learning how to study right the first time. You just learned how to read the right way the first time by power reading, and now we are going to talk about taking notes the right way.

This is how you save yourself time in the long run, and it's how you can manage to pull the grades you want and not be living under a constant cloud of stress.

You've got to set yourself up to succeed from the beginning. Which is why this hack to note-taking is our next power habit.

There really is an art to note-taking, and doing it correctly can not only help you commit the information to memory, it can provide you with a foolproof study outline once midterms and finals roll around.

Of course, you have to actually be in class to take good notes—so let's not forget about our second power habit!

TAKE YOUR OWN NOTES

Nowadays, a lot of professors will provide outlines or lecture notes to their students. Sometimes professors will distribute "guided notes" that have blanks or missing information to help students actively listen and record the missing information during the lecture. These can be quite helpful; however, you may want to enhance any notes you receive by still taking your own.

You may be thinking, *I already have the professor's notes, so why take my own?!?* But the truth is, taking your own notes can actually help solidify those concepts in your brain.

Even if you decide to type those notes out (perhaps because not even you can read your handwriting), there is still a lot to be gained by taking notes yourself. Putting those concepts in your own words, developing a shorthand, and using symbols to do so as you listen in on a lecture, really can help you to connect with, and remember, that material in the long run.

Now, this should go without saying, but once more for the back row, that this step obviously requires you to be present in class. Not just there, but also paying attention and actively participating with as few distractions as possible.

If you need a good method for taking notes, check out the Cornell Notes system online sometime. It's a great, practical way to organize your notes and process them later, and you can even download premade templates for it. Plus, this method already incorporates many of the strategies that I am going to share with you.

Don't get too hung up on what method works best or the "how-to-write-your-notes" part, because the most important thing to remember is to find a system that works for you, make it a routine, and your brain will adapt to it if you use it consistently.

After some practice taking lecture notes, you will improve your speed and accuracy. With even more practice, you will gain a better idea of how to decipher what is important to write down and from what is not, especially since it can be quite subjective and more related to each professor's style of speaking than to any specific tip I could give you. But over time, you'll start to pick up on what's most worth writing down. Until then, try to write as much as you can—recognizing that all professors are prone to tangents and that you certainly aren't responsible for writing down personal anecdotes or random asides.

On the practical side, you want to leave as much of the margin space in your notebook as blank as possible. The Cornell method provides a very practical template for this purpose by creating a left margin that takes up one third of the page, while the note-taking area is provided by the remaining space. Soon you will find that you will be utilizing that margin space just like you do the margins in your textbooks.

The more skilled you become at note-taking (which can only happen with practice), the more efficient your brain will become at recognizing connections and deciphering important material. I truly believe that everyone can train their brain to readily pick up on those connections, actually becoming smarter in the process. And attending each class, actively participating, and taking notes how I've described is exactly the way to begin that training.

REVIEW, REVIEW, REVIEW

Immediately after each class, you should be reviewing the notes you've just taken. This doesn't take long, just a few minutes to look over what you wrote down. But you absolutely want to do this while the information is still fresh in your mind, because doing so will help you to further commit that information to memory.

Even better, if you've got time, use some of your reading strategies to look over those notes. That means grabbing a pen and highlighter to further mark up the notes you've taken in the same way you process your reading material. Plus, you can clarify and clean up anything you may have written a bit too quickly in class.

Reviewing information right after a class is a key step in the learning process, again because the information is still fresh. If anything is really unclear to you or you missed some important information, then now is also the time to write out those questions, or to include a question mark next to the material in the margins. That way, you know to seek out those answers later—either from your book, or perhaps a study group, or by approaching the professor directly.

The next time you sit down to do your reading for that class, you should also review your most recent lecture notes—and attempt to answer any questions you wrote down from those notes. You've already got your book in front of you, after all! And combining a review of your notes with your assigned reading will help you make connections between the two.

Finally, you should do a brief review of those same notes once more before your next class, and I would often do this while walking to class. I realize this may seem like overkill, but the repetition and pre-class refresher are hugely beneficial to learning these concepts. And spending the extra few minutes to look over those notes now will actually save you hours in study time later—I promise!

ANTICIPATE THE TEST QUESTIONS

I'm going to let you in on a little secret: you can absolutely develop the ability to anticipate test questions long before you ever see the exam.

No, I'm not talking about any psychic voodoo here. I'm just talking about using your knowledge base to look for patterns, and to think a bit like your professors while you're at it!

You've already completed high school or had enough experience with it, so you're familiar with the types of information that are most often tested. In fact, we already covered that material in the last chapter, when we discussed what to focus on and highlight as you read. This is the stuff that most often makes it to your exams. I want you to see this list again, because it's that important.

Learning new definitions or specialized terminology

Identifying the main idea of the content

Knowing the what, how, and why of a given topic

Recognizing cause and effect relationships

Recognizing the order of events

Comparing and contrasting two or more things

Understanding and applying the steps to a process or formula

Understanding relationships between topics discussed

Analyzing and synthesizing data

Drawing logical conclusions

Making practical applications to the real world

Making judgments or giving opinions and supporting them with your ideas or facts

Your notes are the perfect place to start anticipating those questions, and to write a few out for you to refer back to later. For instance, a practical example might be to write, "What is the definition of _____?" when new terms are mentioned. By adding and highlighting that question at the end of your notes, or in the margin of where the term is first mentioned, you give yourself a reference point to come back to later.

Remember Bloom's Taxonomy when it comes to generating a good variety of questions. You obviously can't stay at the most superficial level of questioning, which merely recalls basic facts and concepts, and still expect to get a deeper understanding. (See the Bloom's Taxonomy of Educational Learning Objectives on the following page.)

BLOOM'S TAXONOMY OF
EDUCATIONAL LEARNING OBJECTIVES

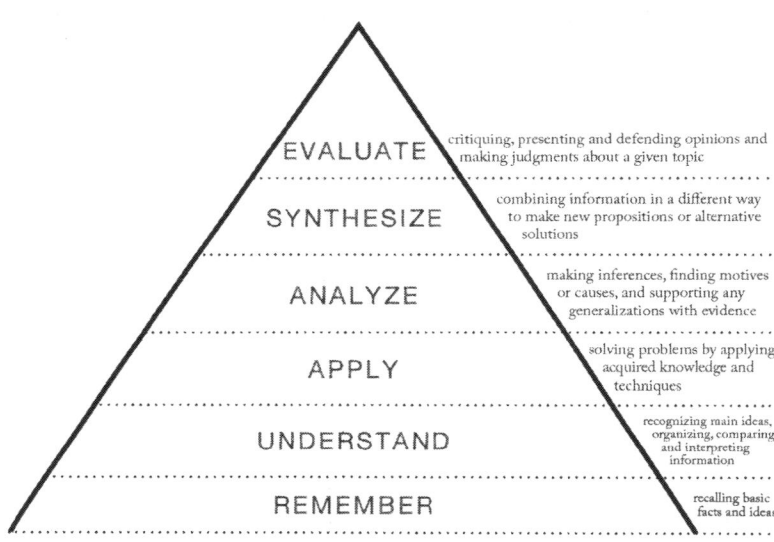

EVALUATE — critiquing, presenting and defending opinions and making judgments about a given topic

SYNTHESIZE — combining information in a different way to make new propositions or alternative solutions

ANALYZE — making inferences, finding motives or causes, and supporting any generalizations with evidence

APPLY — solving problems by applying acquired knowledge and techniques

UNDERSTAND — recognizing main ideas, organizing, comparing and interpreting information

REMEMBER — recalling basic facts and ideas

In general, questions are one of the best ways to activate your brain, so use them to engage your mind and get it focused on what you're studying. Another way to help your brain make some of those necessary connections is to ask yourself questions that may not make it onto your next exam, but can help you understand the concepts that most certainly will be there. Here are a few that can help you make those crucial connections:

"How is this new topic related to everything else that I am learning?"

"Why is this important to know?"

"How does this fit in or connect with everything else I'm learning about this topic?"

You may not know the answers right away; that's fine. Ask yourself anyway, and write the questions down to refer back to later. Your brain will actually continue to work on these questions in your subconscious mind, even when you're not in the midst of studying. And you will be amazed when the answers suddenly pop into your head later.

I have used that technique to correctly answer test questions throughout my college career and post-graduate studies. That is, when I was totally clueless or stumped about a test question, I would actually ask myself that question inside my head, mark it to come back and revisit later, and then just move on with the test. So many times, by just using that technique, the answer would come to me or another piece of information on the test would cue my brain to remember something else that allowed me to figure out the correct answer.

Generating your own test questions makes you think more deeply, and the more you get used to asking questions, the better you'll become at answering them!

CHAPTER SIX ACTION STEPS

1. Take notes in class on each lecture, even if the professor's notes are provided.

2. Review the notes as soon as possible after each class, and process them by clarifying and cleaning them up while they're still fresh in your mind.

3. During your study time, read through your notes again and try to focus on labels, new vocabulary, and making connections to the reading and other lecture material.

4. Try to do a quick review of your notes right before the next class, by arriving early or reviewing them while you're on your way.

5. Learn to anticipate and formulate a good variety of test questions using Bloom's Taxonomy as a guide.

7. THE BRAINCHAT STUDY METHOD

All *The Study Secret* power habits we've discussed up to now? They serve a greater purpose. Yes, they are integral to stepping up your study game, but they are also the prep work for the most important power habit of all.

Understanding and implementing the BrainChat Study Method—the way to study better.

That's right. Everything I've taught you up to now has been leading to this moment. To this power habit.

Can I get a drum roll, please?

The BrainChat Study Method is a collection of top studying practices, developed to accommodate how your brain learns best. Again, this method allows you to successfully process, understand and learn vast amounts of information, not just remember it all for a test. It is an approach based in research, common sense, and real-world experience. And it is about to change the course of your college education.

YOUR BRAIN IS AWESOME

What if I told you that your brain is an incredibly awesome, adaptive and resilient organ? That honestly, if you were to commit yourself fully, your brain could likely find a way to make just about any study method work.

You could figure out how to pass and graduate without the

BrainChat Study Method. But you would probably be working harder and seeing weaker results, because you wouldn't be working in the way your brain prefers. You wouldn't be customizing your study sessions for the most efficient results.

Which means working harder, accomplishing less, and spending far more time studying than socializing.

And no one wants that.

But before you can really understand why the BrainChat Study Method works (and why you should commit to embracing what I'm about to teach you), you need a basic understanding of how the brain works.

One of the first concepts we learn as a child is language. Even before we can speak, we begin understanding that there is a labeling system for every person, place, thing, action, and concept that exists.

That's right. While "I hate labels" has become the rally cry of youth, your brain loves labels. In fact, it thrives off labels and names everything you encounter.

Think about it. Across every country and culture, there are words, compound words, or groups of words to describe everything in existence—no matter how simple or complex a concept may be.

Previously, I put a lot of emphasis on new vocabulary in both the chapters on power reading and hacking your notes. Why? Because learning new vocabulary is at the root of meaningful learning. Some even argue that your vocabulary comprehension is the best measurement of intelligence. The truth is your brain likes to learn new words, which makes paying attention to new words and understanding their definitions fundamental to learning.

These newly discovered word labels are the basic building blocks of knowledge, which your brain then organizes into more complex concepts and ideas, especially the more you utilize them in different contexts.

When you are really young, most of the vocabulary you learn are concrete things that you substantiate with your five senses. But as we grow older, we are introduced to labels that represent more abstract concepts or actions--for example, words like "outer space" or "doing calculus."

If I were to say the word "apple" to you, your brain would immediately conjure up an image of an apple. You might remember the last time you had an apple and be able to recall the smell, taste and even the feel of an apple in your hand. All this background data is organized by your brain so that when you think about the word "apple," or anything associated with apples, that information and those memories are all readily connected and available for recall.

This labeling and organizing of information is really the brain's principal task when it comes to learning. It's all about making those connections that allow the world around us to make sense. And it's how the brain uses old information to construct and learn new knowledge.

That's why it's so important for you to build the blocks of knowledge by learning new vocabulary as you go and correctly processing your lessons into your working memory before moving on to future learning. Because if you don't understand the fundamentals, then learning the information awaiting you at the next step (next chapter, the next course, next semester; whatever it may be) will be even more challenging.

So highlight those vocab words as you come across them, and make sure you understand the words used to define them (if not, look those up, too). They really are key to grasping the concepts you're learning.

I believe the absolute best test to see if you really understand a new word or complex concept is being able to accurately explain it out loud to yourself. If you can do that, then you know you have it down and can move forward.

In fact, one of the best ways to learn new vocabulary is making flashcards. I used flashcards not only to improve my English vocabulary but also to learn four other languages. Flashcards are very effective for making question and answer sets out of material you're studying for almost any other class. Just write the new word on one side and its definition on the other, or questions on one side and the answer on the other. I saw so many of my students excel as a direct result of using flashcards.

Check out different flashcard apps like Cram, Quizlet, or StudyBlue that can help you take even more advantage of those shorter study blocks we talked about earlier, by always having easy access to material to study right on your phone. Remember, those little blocks of time are your secret weapon to catching up and getting ahead.

THE SEVEN LEARNING STYLES

It's also important to understand that not everyone learns in the same way. While I have outlined steps for learning that I truly believe to be important, there is a lot of variation in how people learn best. In fact, there are seven recognized learning styles that have a lot to do with how you process and retain information:

Visual/Spatial: Learners who tend to learn best by seeing and visualizing new information. They like the use of images, charts and graphs, pictures, video, and maps in their learning and typically understand them with ease. Visual learners also take more notice of layout and spatial organization and are drawn to color.

Aural/Auditory: Learners who tend to learn best by listening to new information. They respond well to sound, like rhythm and rhyme, and enjoy music. Auditory learners get more out of lectures, because they are active listeners. They are also more apt to speak up in class and like studying in groups.

Verbal/Linguistic: Learners who tend to prefer learning new information by reading it or writing it; those who don't shy away from lengthy reading or writing assignments. They tend to be avid readers and good writers.

Physical/Kinesthetic: Learners who prefer being actively engaged in the learning process. They prefer to do things, make things, and engage in other hands-on experiences to learn and process new information and skills. They often excel at sports, theater arts, and role-playing.

Logical/Mathematical: Learners who tend towards mathematics, analysis, reasoning, and systems.

Social/Interpersonal: Learners who prefer to interact in groups.

Solitary/Intrapersonal: Learners who prefer to be on their own.

Now, like most personality concepts, there can be a lot of variation between these types. You might be both a visual and kinesthetic learner, aural and logical, or any other combination you might imagine.

But most people have a natural preference towards the way they learn best. Recognizing that preference, and how your brain best learns, can be important for success and allows you to customize the BrainChat Study Method to accommodate your preferences.

Still, no matter what your dominant learning style is, brain research has shown that when we engage as many of the five senses as possible while learning, the brain makes deeper and more lasting connections with the information. Keep that in mind as I introduce you to the BrainChat Study Method, a method designed to engage all the learning styles.

PROPER PREPARATION IS KEY

For the BrainChat Study Method to be most effective, there are a few things you first need to do in preparation:

1. Prioritize what to study.

2. Prepare your study space.

3. Get your mental and emotional faculties ready to study.

When it comes to prioritizing what to study, a general rule of thumb is to focus on what you will be tested on soonest. But if you find yourself needing to study several subjects at once, you should focus on the subject you find most difficult first; mastering harder concepts always takes longer than brushing up on concepts you feel more comfortable with.

Next, you need to prepare your study space, just as we discussed in earlier chapters. Ideally, your study space should be solely dedicated to studying; a spot that your brain doesn't associate with other activities like sleeping or playing video games. It should also be a space where you feel comfortable talking aloud, even if just in a mumble or whisper, as you will occasionally want to read some of your text and notes out loud. Deck this space out with some cool lighting and even a calming scent; lemon, lavender, jasmine, peppermint, cinnamon, and rosemary can all be great essential oils or candle scents to promote studying. It doesn't matter as long as it's pleasant and calming to you.

Finally, you need to prepare your mind for your designated study time. On the physical level this means being well-rested, hydrated, and fueled with healthy snacks. On the psychological level, it means reducing stress and entering your study session in a peaceful, positive frame of mind.

You wouldn't believe how excessive stress and anxiety can nullify a good study session, so use some positive self-talk, a brief timeout to visualize your goals, and deep breaths as needed to relax and signal to your brain that you're ready to learn.

Before you begin, quickly survey the amount of material that you need to cover from your notes, and then divide that into smaller, more manageable parts. Give yourself stopping points where you can take quick brain breaks.

Now, you're ready to begin!

THE BRAINCHAT STUDY METHOD IN THREE PHASES

Studying, and I mean really studying, is all about seeing the big picture, making connections with the important details, and developing a deeper understanding of the content. For this reason, you need to go back over your notes and the chapters in your book they correlate with. It's about reviewing what you've already written and read, and making connections as you do.

I'm not talking about re-reading the 200 pages assigned to you in the last month and that you already completed. Instead, I'm talking about reviewing all the notes you personally took, along with the margin notes and questions you wrote there, as well as the highlighted sections you created in your books. This is something you should do section by section, with your notes and books alongside each other.

For the first phase of the BrainChat Study Method, begin your reading silently. Well, read everything silently *except* the topic headings, subheadings, and any important titles or labels you come across. Those should all be read out loud (even if it's just a mumble that you alone can hear), because remember, your brain loves labels. And headings and subheadings are usually "big-idea-type" labels that your brain especially likes, because it always wants to organize information and connect that information to something.

By reading those out loud, you are giving those big-idea labels added emphasis in your brain, and keeping your mind better focused as you progress through the reading.

If you didn't get to review your notes right after class, then you also need to use this first pass through your notes to write any potential test questions in the margins.

Feel free to enhance your notes during this first phase of study. Add to them or draw arrows to visually emphasize and represent those invisible connections that your brain needs to make. You should also underline or highlight key words and important concepts or topics that were emphasized in class and that you may have overlooked before. You may even need to make corrections to something you noticed was initially recorded incorrectly, misunderstood, or misspelled.

While you're studying, always immediately look up any words in the reading or notes that you don't know the meaning of. Again, expanding your vocabulary is one of the best things you can do to make yourself smarter.

Don't get too wrapped up in how your notes look at this point. They may be a bit messy (okay, really messy), especially with your margin notes, highlighted content, drawings, and arrows pointing to all the connections and relationships; but this just shows you're working to make those connections in the first place. With practice, you'll make this process your own and develop a more custom functional format for yourself—which usually involves knowing just how much space to leave yourself both in the margins and between topics.

Now, before you ever sit down to review this material, you should have established stopping points, by mentally breaking it down into smaller sections. When you get to those stopping points, evaluate how you're feeling and either take a short break or decide to power through to the next stopping point. Because that is something you can do— you're allowed to keep going if your brain is still feeling fresh.

Of course, you can also use those breaks to reward yourself with small distractions. You should have your phone on silent and out of sight, but maybe after you finish studying this section, you can take five minutes to stand up and walk to where you left it. Reward yourself with the opportunity to reply to a text or check your email. We're all so hyper-connected these days, so depriving yourself of that connection and allowing it only when you reach certain study milestones can be a powerful motivator.

Keep those brain breaks short, though. No more than five to ten minutes at a time. Save bigger rewards, like going to the movies with your friends or playing a video game, for when your entire study session is over.

Developing this habit of delayed gratification is crucial to your future success, as there will always be more desires to gratify than our time and resources allow. Plus, allowing yourself rewards can help you to learn self-discipline, which will come in handy in so many other aspects of your life down the road.

With time and practice, you will build up your brain's capacity to process and learn greater quantities of information, as well as increase your study stamina by being able to take on longer study times between breaks. But you need to follow this format until you have completely studied all your notes.

Unfortunately, this is where most students stop.

You know better, though. It's time for Phase Two.

PHASE TWO

After going through your notes once alongside your books, Phase Two requires you to review those same notes once more, only this time in a much quicker manner. The whole purpose of this phase is to allow repetition to commit those notes to your working memory.

Again, you need to read the topic headings out loud, just as you did before, and read any questions that you may have written in the margins out loud, as well. You should also be able to answer those questions as you go now. If you can't, dedicate some time to those individual concepts until you can.

All the processing you did in Phase One helped your brain further organize and comprehend this information with all the pertinent details. With this second reading, you will definitely have a better basic understanding of all the content and you should start to have what I call a "big picture" realization, which is just a general understanding of how all the information is related and weaves together. There is always a "big picture" to be seen, and another way to find it is to read over an outline of the notes or outline of the textbook chapters. These outlines can make that realization clearer. A lot of planning goes into the order, structure, and layout of both your textbooks and professor's lecture notes, so it's there. You just have to look for it.

During Phase Two, your brain will make deeper connections.

And it's common for more lightbulbs to come on in your mind, when you suddenly see things that you did not see or understand so clearly before.

Moreover, since you have now seen this material a few times, your mind will actually begin to anticipate what's next as you read through the information, remembering what you wrote and what comes next. That's important and it's what you want to happen.

At some point during this phase, all the information should start to feel more fluid for you, allowing you to think about, process, and remember what you're reading with significantly more ease. That flowing feel to the information is the signal that your brain is ready for Phase Three. If you don't have that flow, and if the information still feels hard to remember, choppy, or disjointed, then you need to repeat Phase Two again until it feels vivid and connected.

I know that can seem frustrating, and for many students, it can be hard to stay motivated through multiple readings through your notes. However, as a word of encouragement to press on, this phase is only hard in the beginning, meaning that as you embrace this study method and utilize it, each time you study, your brain will actually begin to process and learn things faster, knowing what you expect of it.

In other words, there is a compound effect with the BrainChat Study Method, meaning that your brain also learns this study method, understands what is expected in each phase, and then adapts its processing to apply this strategy in an ongoing manner to the new material you're learning.

So I'm telling you, if you can push through, it gets easier and easier. And that's when you really start to reap the rewards of using it.

But Phase Three is where the deepest learning and greatest transfer into long-term memory occurs.

Phase Three is all about *mastery!*

PHASE THREE

This is the phase that's most crucial for the BrainChat Study

Method. It's also the step that separates this study method from most other common study methods, because in this phase, you actually become the teacher.

You will now use your notes to teach and explain the material to yourself out loud (or with a study buddy or study group, whatever you prefer).

Yes, it has to be out loud. You do not have to do this in a formal tone, as if you're giving a lecture, but just explain the content as though you were teaching a friend, still using all your new vocabulary, but in simple terms. The goal of this phase is to use your notes as a mere reference point as you go through each topic and teach it to yourself, or practice teaching one another in group study.

You should be asking and answering your questions, describing the main ideas and concepts, and detailing examples; all while trying not to look at your notes so much. At this level, the information should flow to you and you should be able to explain new definitions, key concepts, and relationships within the content with relative ease. Don't be surprised if you see some even deeper connections as you go.

Now, let me clarify: The goal of this phase is not to have memorized your notes, but rather to have synthesized the information in a way that allows you to readily verbalize what you've already processed and learned. Memorization is not the same as meaningful learning, and some students mistakenly think it is. That being said, the BrainChat Study Method is great for memorizing information, because it gives you a systematic approach for doing so. However, memorizing information and having a fundamental understanding of that same information are two distinct things.

The one key step in this phase is to keep asking yourself anything that you have trouble readily explaining until you can accurately do so without looking at your notes at all for help. The ultimate test to whether you understand something is hearing yourself explain it out loud. If you struggle putting your explanation into words, then you don't have it yet. So look down at those notes and keep repeating what you're missing until you've got it. Otherwise, we often convince ourselves that we have something down and completely understand it when we actually don't.

Everyone knows repetition is good for the brain, but repetition in this phase is even better, because it's repetition with a deeper understanding behind it. So keep repeating anything that gives you trouble, before you go on to the next topic.

This step is crucial because you want your brain to hear yourself correctly explain everything and accurately answer all the questions that you've asked. All of this talking to your brain is where the BrainChat Study Method gets its name.

In short, if you can teach a topic to yourself verbally, then you understand it at a mastery level.

WHY IS THE BRAINCHAT STUDY METHOD SO EFFECTIVE?

Mel Silberman, a well-known psychologist who pioneered research in the areas of interpersonal intelligence and active learning, wrote the following in his book, *Active Learning: 101 Strategies to Teach Any Subject*:

What I hear, I forget.
What I hear and see, I remember a little.
What I hear, see, and ask questions about or discuss with someone else, I begin to understand.
What I hear, see, discuss, and do, I acquire knowledge and skill.
What I teach to another, I master (1996, p.1)

This is the secret behind the BrainChat Study Method—the fact that it engages multiple senses and faculties of your body in the process of learning.

First, you are physically touching the notes as you read them, and your pen and highlighter as you add more notes, underline, write questions, and draw arrows. Your brain is having to process the tactile stimulation and coordinate all of those movements.

At the same time, you are using your eyes to read the words while your mind makes sense of and processes what you are reading. In order to ask and develop questions, you are having to process and synthesize the information even further and make judgments about what format might be best to test your understanding of the content.

In all three phases of the BrainChat Study Method, you are also reading things out loud, which simultaneously engages your sight, speaking ability and hearing. As you advance to Phase Three and teach yourself or someone else, your brain must recall the information and then properly formulate words to put it into intelligible speech.

While you hear your explanation, you are making judgments about how you sound and whether you are using the right words to accurately explain the concepts and the answers to your questions. If not, then your brain is having to instantaneously problem-solve and decide what is incorrect, where to find the accurate information and how to restate it correctly.

All of this stimulation lights your brain up with meaningful learning activity.

After consistently applying the three phases of the BrainChat Study Method, it becomes a powerful study regimen or routine. But you really need to make this method your own and adapt it to work for you. It's a great study system that you should customize by incorporating methods you know have worked for you in the past and that cater to your learning style.

You can customize this method to meet your individual learning needs, getting the most out of the BrainChat Study Method in the process. A personal customization for me (probably related to the kinesthetic learner in me) is incorporating hand gestures or even acting out things in my notes. For example, when I was reciting lists of things, then I would make a "one," "two," "three," and so on using my fingers as I spoke them. If I was comparing and contrasting two things, then I might actually stand up in a spot to the left and state the exclusive characteristics of the first item, and then walk over to another spot to the right and state those of the second item followed by standing in the middle of those two spots to state what they had in common, as if I were acting out a Venn Diagram. I didn't do these things every time, but more when the material was particularly difficult or I needed to change it up a bit to stay engaged.

In my experience, it's best to do your required reading and after-class note reviews during those small blocks of time that we discussed earlier. Then you can utilize your larger blocks of study time for the second and third phases of the BrazinChat Study Method.

Now, even if you're a social learner, I recommend completing the first and second phases alone. You need to study by yourself to get the basics down first—you'll be more useful to a study group and gain more from those sessions if you do.

Phase Three is great for studying in groups. Of course, it helps if your study group is also utilizing the BrainChat Study Method! Otherwise, you will just stand out as a superstar each time.

When and how you choose to study is ultimately up to you. Just make sure you prioritize well so that you get everything covered throughout the semester; you don't want to be stuck cramming right before exams. And if you apply this method consistently, you won't ever have to cram again.

STUDYING FOR MIDTERM AND FINAL EXAMS

Now, I realize the BrainChat Study Method sounds like it involves a fair amount of work. And let's be honest, it does. But I promised you this study method will save you time—valuable time that you can then commit to social activities (or whatever else you choose to do with your time). Here's how.

Students who don't know how to study correctly often find themselves panicking as exams approach. They have no system. This is when they cram, when they lock themselves into dorm rooms, or practically move into the library, and spend the days leading up to exams reading and reviewing everything they can get their hands on.

The problem is, they're exhausted and aren't retaining information all that well. Plus, they're reviewing content they wouldn't have had to review at all if they had taken adequate notes and utilized the BrainChat Study Method shortly after taking those notes.

This method saves you hours of study time when you have to study for mid-term exams and final exams. In fact, when that time comes, I prescribe starting with a quick read-through of all your notes, again, by manageable chunks. Do this with the view of primarily stimulating and activating your brain to tap into those areas where these topics and concepts are stored in your memory. Have different colored highlighters handy and use color-coordinated dots or circle information that was on prior tests or quizzes.

While we're on that topic, you should always look at your quizzes and tests to analyze what you missed and understand why you got it wrong. If you honestly don't know why you got something wrong, then make it a point to discuss that with your professor. And always keep your old quizzes and exams if your professors return them to you; these can be great to review prior to midterms and finals.

After a quick review, go through your notes once more with a Phase Three focus. Simply mark the areas you don't get on a first pass, and spend some additional time focusing on those areas after your Phase Three review.

In doing this, you've highlighted the few areas you need to study harder, and now you know with certainty where to spend your valuable study time. More importantly, you eliminate the need to cram and you'll stop wasting time studying all the stuff you already know well.

Again, how do you know that you know it well enough? You know it if you can verbally explain it out loud to yourself. The "out loud" part is the crucial test that makes Phase Three unique, because if you cannot do it out loud, then you instantly realize this fact as you stumble to find the words. This way there is no fooling your brain.

If you don't do it out loud, then you will fall into the common trap of thinking you know the material well enough when you actually don't. That is exactly what most students do, and why you are going to stand out.

You know what else is cool about doing everything out loud?

You already have the academic language organized in your mind to answer any type of questions, even short-answer and essay-type questions, too. So this study method works with whatever way you are being tested. Even so, I still recommend making an outline of what points you will cover on any essay-type questions, especially if you already know what they will be.

CHAPTER SEVEN ACTION STEPS

1. Utilize your small blocks of time to do quick after-class reviews of your notes and start any assigned reading.

2. Maximize your big blocks of time to do a Phase Two study of your class notes, until you sense the easy flow of information and then complete your Phase Three pass for mastery of the material.

3. If possible, always analyze your old quizzes and exams to see what you missed and why. If permitted, keep these for later reference and preparation for studying for any midterms or finals.

4. If you study in a group, be sure to set expectations for all the members to at least do the required reading and a Phase One pass through the notes before the study group meets.

8. SEEK A BALANCED LIFE

I've spent the bulk of this book talking about studying, which makes sense, since it's a book about powerful study habits. But I want to end with the last *Study Secret* power habit that is just as important—seeking a balanced life, because without balance, you can't find success in any realm of your life. Not just while you are in college but even afterwards. In fact, without balance, you don't have it all.

Certainly not academically.

I believe that one of the most important responsibilities we have in life is properly caring for our personal health and wellness. Unfortunately, the college years are a time when this priority is often taken for granted. You're young and feel invincible. Plus, you're being pulled in a hundred different directions all at once. So it can be easy to place self-care on the back burner.

But that doesn't mean you should.

Trust me, I get it. Remember, I was a college student once myself. I was even a frat guy, and I'm fully aware of all that entails.

But the poor life habits you form during this stage of your early adulthood can not only hinder your academic success, they can have devastating effects on your overall health and wellness for many years to come. That compound effect works not only positively, but also negatively; your physical body and emotional well-being can face long-term consequences just as easily as they can reap rewards. It all depends on the choices you make.

For this reason, you want to make sure your life habits are actually helping you achieve your goals and not sabotaging your efforts.

Remember, there are very few problems in life that developing a new habit or getting rid of an old one won't solve.

Take a minute to think about the activities in life that are literally keeping you going—breathing, drinking, eating, sleeping and exercising. Good habits in these areas are so crucial to learn and practice during your college years. So let's just look briefly at each one.

First, take a deep breath right now, breathing through your nose. Hold it for one or two seconds, and then slowly release it through your mouth, while visualizing letting go of all that stress and tension in your body.

Doesn't that feel good?

Let's face it: Life is super stressful at times, and deep breathing is great for calming your mind and body. That's why it is especially useful right before you study, take a test, or begin a class lecture, because it also acts as a signal to your brain to change gears and refocus on the task at hand. Use this to your advantage, and make deep breathing a habit you dedicate time to every day.

Second, water is essential to life. It is common knowledge that our bodies are composed mostly of water, about 60% in the average adult. There are numerous reasons to keep yourself properly hydrated to maintain good health. But how do you know if you're drinking enough water?

A simple self-test that a doctor gave me was to gently rub your lips together. They should generally feel moist and smooth. But if they feel even slightly dry, rough or coarse, then you need to drink more water. So if you are not carrying a water bottle around with you, then go get one and make this a new habit.

Third, now that you're in college, you may be making more choices about what you eat, especially if you are no longer living at home. I definitely recommend an on-campus meal plan if available, for three main reasons: It's very convenient, the variety of food choices, and it saves a lot of time. Even so, you will most likely need to prepare some of your own meals at times and keep some healthy snacks on hand.

Try to stay away from junk food and fast foods as much as possible (which I realize are a staple of college life, but don't have to be) and instead aim for eating a healthy, whole-foods diet. WebMD published an online article by Carol Sorgen called, "Eat Smart for a Healthier Brain" which highlights several great super foods that can boost your brain power. These include blueberries, wild salmon, nuts and seeds, avocados, whole grains, colorful fruits and vegetables, beans, pomegranate juice, freshly brewed tea, and even dark chocolate (December 18, 2008). You won't always have the metabolism you have today, and taking care of your body now isn't just good for your brain; it's also good for the image you're going to see in the mirror 10 years from now!

Next, you need to make sleep a priority. Depending on your age, your needs differ, but it is generally recognized that most adults need seven to eight hours of sleep each night. If you're younger (late teens), you need even more.

Many research studies have demonstrated that getting less than six hours, even for just one night, can result in poor brain function. More specifically, it can impair both short-term and long-term memory recall, as well as hindering various cognitive functions and cognitive-related behaviors. We're talking about attention span, the ability to focus or concentrate, cognitive speed, and basic decision-making capacity.

Look, I know you want to go to that party. Or stay out with your friends all night, just because. Things are going to come up, and you're going to have amazing nights that lead into exhausted days. That's life, and it's certainly part of college life.

But it's all about finding a balance. About getting that full night's rest as often as you possibly can, and recognizing that not every social activity is worth sacrificing that sleep.

Because let's face it, some nights out are lamer than others.

So make a commitment to yourself to be in bed by a certain

time at least five nights a week. And make it more if nothing truly worth that sleep deprivation is going on.

And let's be honest, from a health and brain standpoint—very little is worth that sleep deprivation. But I get that from a social standpoint, that line becomes blurred.

Again, in a word: balance.

Lastly, it's important to make regular exercise a part of your lifestyle, as well. Most colleges make it easier by including a gym membership as a part of your enrollment. You're paying for it, so you might as well use it.

Exercise is good for your whole body, your self-image, reduces stress, and slows the effects of aging. If you have never made regular exercise part of your weekly schedule, take action and do it now. Find a friend as a workout buddy and help each other. If you already exercise, then use your college years to get in the best shape of your life and stay active.

But remember . . . balance.

Let that be the driving force throughout your college years and beyond. Balance. Balance in your social activities, balance in work commitments, and balance in how you push yourself forward.

Set your goals, and keep those goals at the forefront of your mind. Spend time with your friends and family, and enjoy all the social opportunities college has to offer. Get to know who you are and what you want out of life.

But always strive for that balance. And remember where your priorities reside. Keep your eye on the prize—that college degree. And if anything else in your life starts to distract you from that goal, reevaluate and reset your sights on balance.

CHAPTER EIGHT ACTION STEPS

1. Practice deep breathing to de-stress and refocus your attention and energy right before your class lectures, study sessions and tests.

2. Take a water bottle with you and keep yourself well-hydrated.

3. Incorporate as many of the super foods mentioned in your diet as possible. Start by adding one or two as daily snacks. If you don't immediately see any super foods you like, go online to find others.

4. Aim to get seven to eight hours of sleep each night, depending on your age and body's needs.

5. Make a strong commitment to regular exercise. A great place to start is working up to 30 minutes of aerobic exercise at least four times per week.

6. Make sure your recreation and social activities are ones that keep you on the path toward your education goals and not sabotaging your efforts. Be mature enough to make changes if necessary.

9. PUTTING IT ALL TOGETHER

I almost wish you could put this book down and come back to read this final chapter after you've been consistently implementing all the power habits with the BrainChat Study Method and experienced some success with them.

Why? Because there are some very important lessons and benefits that you reap from putting these methods into action and experiencing firsthand the compound effect that results from their synergy while you're going to college.

Earlier in the book, I mentioned that you could reap unimaginable benefits from going to college and getting a degree—any degree really. The truth is that going to college and finishing a degree changes you. For most people, you truly become a better version of yourself.

I hope most of you are familiar with classic movie *The Karate Kid*. If not the original, then at least the remake. If you are, you may remember that the premise centers on a kid named Daniel, who is getting bullied and turns to his neighbor, Mr. Miyagi, to teach him karate.

He's desperate for lessons and even agrees to do chores for Mr. Miyagi in exchange for those lessons. Mr. Miyagi gives him a series of seemingly random tasks, like waxing his car and painting the fence around his whole backyard. He carefully demonstrates to Daniel how to do each chore correctly, using very specific techniques. Daniel does the chores but begins to think that Mr.

Miyagi is never going to teach him any karate.

When he hits a breaking point and wants to quit, that's when Mr. Miyagi explains that Daniel has already learned karate; the moves that he demonstrated in how to paint the fence and wax the car were actually karate moves used to effectively block attacks. He throws punches at Daniel while yelling "wax on, wax off" and "paint the fence," and Daniel uses the moves he learned doing the chores to successfully deflect the punches. In repeating all those actions so many times, he actually learned valuable karate moves without even realizing it.

Well, practicing the eight power habits during your college experience will have a similar result. The compound effect of doing them day after day causes some interesting things to happen, things that actually start to mold who you are, even in subtle, intangible ways you might not recognize at first.

Let me explain . . .

THE COMPOUND EFFECT OF THE STUDY SECRET

First, by learning to make plans, you have to thoughtfully consider what you want to accomplish, and what resources are necessary to carry out your plans. This helps train your brain to think ahead before it acts. In order to make plans, you have to identify what your goals are, and you now know how goals give direction and purpose to your actions, especially when you write them down.

When you live your life with definite direction and purpose, taking action toward your goals, people who interact with you can sense that you are different in a positive way—that you're clearer about what you want in life. Moreover, your college success plan is easily adaptable to any other type of success plan you want in your life. And because you are a more effective person in general, people will look up to you as a leader.

Second, by going to every class, you have established a habit of showing up no matter what. It required discipline, which you have now gained through your concentrated commitment.

You forced yourself to get up on time, get ready and presentable, and follow through on your assignments. You studied for the quizzes, did the projects and took the tests. You learned about your professor, how he or she presented material, their style of teaching, their expectations--and you adapted your routine accordingly. You had a big workload and you worked through it by breaking it down into smaller parts, learned how to work in groups with people you like and people you didn't like, delegated tasks, utilized others' strengths and covered their weaknesses. You did what needed to be done to complete projects on time.

Did you know that employers are looking for exactly those traits in the people they hire? They are looking for employees who show up for work every day, even when they don't feel like it. For employees who are reliable, teachable, and know how to successfully work with others. They seek out people who know how to adapt to a changing environment, aren't afraid to ask questions, and effectively communicate and coordinate with others on projects. They want to hire people who know how to successfully multi-task and problem-solve effectively.

And by going to college, and successfully earning that degree by implementing all the power habits with the BrainChat Study Method, you have molded yourself into just that.

Third, you got to know your professors and learned to talk to them. You confronted your fears and opinions about talking to professors and reaped the rewards for doing so. This helped you learn how to make good first impressions and begin networking within an educational community and at a professional level. In fact, your professors may continue to be a valuable resource for you even after you graduate.

Interactions with your professors gave you multiple opportunities to embrace the mature mindset and use the mature voice to make requests, negotiate, and make your ideas known. You probably started using that same mindset and voice with your parents, and maybe even your friends, and you reaped rewards from those interactions, as well. And yeah, you guessed it: It's the same one you are going to successfully use with your future employers. Everyone can tell you're growing up, and they are proud of you.

In addition, you learned your professors' varied expectations and how to meet them and, even more importantly, how to exceed them. With luck, you had some really good professors, and even a few bad ones, so that you could see and learn from negative examples, too. That mirrors real life.

You learned that some people are difficult to work with and understand, but that you still have to learn to do it in order to get your work done and fulfill your responsibilities. It's hard, but you learned to adapt.

Fourth, by scheduling your time, you learned to look ahead, make a plan, break it down, and estimate your workload. You now know that what gets scheduled is what gets done. And you experienced the power of routines and procedures.

You also learned to adapt to a changing environment, because life happens and throws us all off at times. You know what it's like to be both ahead of and behind schedule, and what it takes to catch up when you do fall behind. You learned how to estimate how much time it would take to complete certain tasks, and you were right on at times and grossly misjudged others. But you have a much better understanding of your abilities—both your strengths and weaknesses.

You learned to prioritize and make good choices about how to use your time most effectively. But you also made some bad decisions and faced those consequences. You learned from your mistakes, which also empowered and motivated you to make better choices going forward. You know how to overcome your procrastination, which has made you more productive, responsible and mature. Now you know that you can do so much more when you have a schedule and can break things down into smaller more manageable tasks.

Next, doing all the assigned reading taught you to pay the price and do things the right way the first time; otherwise, it ends up costing so much more extra time and effort later. You learned that the things in life that are worthwhile often require a lot of time and effort, which only further strengthened your discipline and resolve.

You probably learned how to read faster from so much practice, and you certainly learned how to read *better*. Forcing yourself to do the reading helped you learn how to power read in a way that facilitated your brain in absorbing knowledge, formulating new ideas of your own, making judgments and deciding which concepts are most important.

But most importantly, you learned to see relationships and make meaningful connections. You now know the importance of making those connections, because that is learning. These are all skills that will help you in life, no matter what field of work or study you choose.

All the assigned reading also exposed you to formal academic language, the language that books are written in, the kind of language people use in business. You vastly increased your vocabulary and added hundreds of new words and concepts to your repertoire of knowledge. All this exposure and all of those papers you had to write have made you an effective communicator, as well.

Your intellectual capital has increased immensely, and you have become a smarter, more interesting person, even a better conversationalist. That, too, is going to be useful to you for the rest of your life.

Then, taking notes taught you to be a discerning listener, which is a great character trait.

Having to listen and simultaneously write or type everything you heard trained your brain to multi-task, and practicing that activity for hundreds of classroom lectures actually trained your brain to work faster and more efficiently. Your mental capacity has increased substantially and it's simply easier for you to figure things out and learn new ideas and skills.

You learned how to see relationships and make meaningful connections between the assigned reading and classroom notes that you took, especially when you saw and understood the big picture and how the details related to it. You now look for the big picture in everything as a habit.

Furthermore, you learned how to study those notes effectively by emphasizing proper labels as headings and subheadings. This way your brain could organize the content better, as well as, recognize new vocabulary and important concepts, and turn that information into good questions. Then, of course, you were able to answer those questions correctly.

Learning and implementing the three phases of the BrainChat Study Method trained your brain to study large amounts of information systematically—to understand and learn it, not just hold on to it for a single test. All that talking to yourself has vastly improved your ability to verbalize your ideas, making you a more interesting person to talk to in the process and perhaps even a little more comfortable speaking in front of others.

You found a system that worked for you, and you will look for systems to help you maximize your efforts in whatever you choose going forward.

Now and in the future, you're going to see that *The Study Secret* helped increase your brain's capacity for information (and, I hope, stirred up your desire to learn even more). You will be a better thinker and faster problem-solver as a result, no matter what you're doing. You will be the kind of person who can learn new information quickly and finds making connections automatic.

It's not an easy method, but it is a highly effective one.

As the months and years go by, as you build up that compound effect of implementing these power habits and find that life balance that works for you, you're going to realize you gained all of this, and so much more, from going to college and earning that degree.

You see this is the real reason you're going to college: not just to get a degree, but to be processed, to be refined, to become a better version of yourself. All these results I've mentioned here should be what a "good college education" entails for everyone. Just know that many future employers don't really care what you studied in college as much as they care that you have learned what these crucial skills that the eight power habits produce in you.

Each of these skills will easily transfer to other parts of your life to make you a more effective person overall, even if you end up doing something totally unrelated to what you studied. That's precisely why you should never see getting a college education as a waste.

All of this is why I wish you could put this book down and read this section later, after you've had time to witness the compound effect and tremendous synergy of practicing the eight power habits for yourself.

But instead, I'll just have to settle for saying … stick with it. I promise, you will be so glad you did. And your future will be so much brighter for it!

Just remember that nothing in this book will work unless you do. Nothing great in life is ever achieved without commitment and taking action. I believe in your ability to achieve your goals, and I know you can do it. But this has to be *your* belief, and *you* have to be committed to taking action to reach them.

Everything I've shared with you in *The Study Secret* will help you do that. It will help establish a routine for success, and the eight power habits will follow you and prove useful throughout your brighter future.

What happens now is up to you!

<u>CHAPTER NINE ACTION STEPS</u>

1. Remember that implementing the ideas and techniques in *The Study Secret* is like learning a new exercise workout. You're going to need a few weeks of practicing it before you start to see the results, so go into it with that mentality. Start by reading the chapters of this book that you found to be most helpful at least two more times. You will see deeper connections and internalize the material much better now that you have a big picture overview and general understanding of the ideas presented in the whole book.

2. Start slow, and add one or two habits to your routine and then build up from there.

3. Pay it forward and share what you have learned and the benefits that you have reaped from this book with others.

THE THREE PHASES OF THE BRAINCHAT STUDY METHOD

PHASE ONE

1. Break your notes down into smaller sections and establish some stopping points before you start your study session.

2. If you have assigned reading from textbooks that correlates with your class notes, then read only the highlighted and processed portions, especially any portions that are also covered or emphasized in your notes.

3. Read your class notes silently, except for major topic headings and subheadings and any new vocabulary, which you want to read out loud for emphasis.

4. Start processing your notes by highlighting any new vocabulary and their definitions as well as other key information so that it stands out. Be sure to look up any words you do not readily understand.

5. Continue processing your notes by creating representations using symbols, drawings, pictures, arrows, acronyms, etc. as you go through the material to indicate the unseen connections that you are making in your mind while you read.

6. Write any potential test questions in the margins, keeping Blooms Taxonomy in mind so that you use a wide variety of

questions requiring more complex answers than merely recalling basic facts.

PHASE TWO

1. After completing a reading of your notes once alongside your textbooks, then begin re-reading the notes again. Continue to read all the subject headings aloud and any questions that you have written in the margin. You should also be able to answer those questions before you move on in the material.

2. As you read, be actively thinking about what the "big-picture idea" is and how all the information is related to it. Pose this question to your mind and even see your reading as the unfolding of that answer. Nearly all books and lectures are organized in such a manner to always have a "big-picture idea" in the same way that all the puzzle pieces of a jigsaw puzzle eventually make a big picture. You may have already seen it in Phase One, but it should become clearer in Phase Two.

3. You should read through your notes multiple times until all the information starts to feel more fluid for you, allowing you to think about, process, and remember what you're reading with significantly more ease. Your mind will actually begin to anticipate what's next as you read through the information, remembering what you wrote and even what comes next. That flowing feel to the information is the signal that your brain is ready for Phase Three. If you don't have that flow, and if the information still feels hard to remember, choppy, or disjointed, then you need to repeat Phase Two again until it feels vivid and connected.

PHASE THREE

1. You will now use your notes to teach and explain the material to yourself out loud (or with a study buddy or study group, whatever you prefer). The goal of this phase is to use your notes as a mere reference point that you briefly glance at as you go through each topic and teach it to yourself, or practice teaching one another in group study.

2. The one key step in this phase is to keep asking yourself anything that you have trouble readily explaining until you can accurately do so without looking at your notes at all for help. The ultimate test to whether you understand something is hearing yourself explain it out loud. If you struggle putting your explanation into words, then you don't have it yet. So look down at those notes and keep repeating what you're missing until you've got it.

Made in the USA
Columbia, SC
16 June 2018